Reconciliation: Sacrament With a Future

Reconciliation:
Sacrament With a Future

Sandra DeGidio, O.S.M.

To Mary Alice, from whose patient listening, compassionate forgiveness and gentle nudges I learned the real meaning of "soul friend."

Nihil Obstat: Rev. Hilarion Kistner, O.F.M.
Rev. John J. Jennings

Imprimi Potest: Rev. Jeremy Harrington, O.F.M.
Provincial

Imprimatur: +James H. Garland, V.G.
Archdiocese of Cincinnati
November 20, 1985

The *nihil obstat* and *Imprimatur* are a declaration that a book or pamphlet is considered to be free from doctrinal or moral error. It is not implied that those who have granted the *nihil obstat* and *imprimatur* agree with the contents, opinions or statements expressed.

Book design and cover by Julie Lonneman.

SBN 0-86716-053-5

Contents

Contents

Introduction

Whenever two or more Catholics are gathered together, sooner or later jokes and horror stories about Confession will be told.

Confession, or the Sacrament of Reconciliation as it is called today, is perhaps the most frequent butt of jokes among Catholics and non-Catholics alike. Perhaps the most misunderstood of the seven ritual sacraments of the Church, it is also a major stumbling block for those seeking to know more about the Catholic Church and, at best, a "friendly foe" for many Catholics.

We all have our Confession horror stories—complete with stomach flip-flops, racing heartbeat, panic that the next person in line might have heard one of our worst sins, the fear of forgetting a sin or (God help us) of sinning again between Saturday afternoon's Confession and Sunday morning's Mass. Some might say we are *inordinately* attached to these Confession "horrors."

Why do we carry around this excess baggage, unpacking and displaying it whenever the appropriate opportunity presents itself? Maybe it's because this baggage, no matter how heavy and cumbersome, really comes in handy if we use it right: It provides an excuse for avoiding the Sacrament in our present adult lives.

We must admit, in all candor, that many of us greeted the recent reforms of the Sacrament of Penance with relief—not so much because we understood the theology, but because we thought we found in the new Rite a rationale for confessing less frequently. Of course, we were already doing that anyway, but now we gave ourselves "permission" to do it.

Whenever two or more Church professionals (bishops, priests and unordained Church ministers) are gathered together, sooner or later garments are rent and the fact bewailed that increasing numbers of Catholics are avoiding Confession.

This rending and wailing brought forth the new Rite of Penance that was promulgated by the Congregation for Divine Worship in 1973. The Rite was made available in English in the United States in Advent of 1975, and was mandated to be used in all parishes in this country by the First Sunday of Lent, 1977. Not only did the Rite present us with new formats, rubrics and prayers, more importantly, it gave us a renewed theology of the Sacrament in a 20-page Introduction.

I have a feeling that many Church professionals naively believed that the new Rite—with its emphasis on reconciliation rather than penance, and its comfortable, cheerful reconciliation rooms replacing the old, dark telephone-booth-type confessionals—would produce a massive return to the Sacrament. That didn't happen, and the rending and wailing among Church professionals continued.

So in 1983 bishops representing every country in the world gathered in Rome for the Seventh International Synod of Bishops to discuss and make recommendations regarding "Reconciliation and Penance in the Mission of the Church." In addition, they grappled with the unpopular notion of social sin and its link with sacramental forgiveness and reconciliation. The bishops' insights, though widely reported in the Catholic press, didn't exactly cause a stampede to the reconciliation room.

Whenever two or more analysts of the Catholic scene put thoughts on paper, sooner or later books and articles appear that pessimistically decry the near demise of the Sacrament of Reconciliation.

The Catholic laity, they say, have "waged a quiet revolution" simply by staying away from the Sacrament. And these same authors usually proceed to offer neatly categorized reasons why Catholics have stopped going to Confession. Those reasons range from "I can go directly to God for forgiveness" to "I've been embarrassed and hurt by priests who told me not to waste their time with my trivial sins."

Other frequently cited reasons include:

• Catholics don't consider sin prevalent in their lives anymore. They no longer have an awareness of sin.

• Most Catholics have come to believe that serious sin is very difficult to commit, and since Confession is *legally* required only for serious sin, there is no reason to go.

• Catholics have lost their sense of humility, penance and simplicity because of materialism, consumerism and egoism.

• Lay Catholics have lost confidence in their parish priests' ability to understand and be compassionate about their real-life situations.

• Catholics do not see penance, compassion, kindness and reconciliation exemplified by their parish priests.

• Many Catholics have had abysmally bad experiences in the confessional at one time or another and are afraid to risk the same thing happening again.

• For Catholics who oppose Church teachings on contemporary issues such as contraception, nuclear war, or political involvement of clerics and religious, Confession seems to be an exercise in futility: They perceive their Church leaders as ineffectual and therefore dismiss hierarchical credibility in relation to the sacrament.

• The new Rite of Reconciliation is seldom practiced by either parishioners or parish priests; therefore, it must not be meeting the needs of Catholics today.

Maybe you recognize some of your own words and feelings in the above statements. We can suggest all sorts of reasons for not celebrating the Sacrament—and we have. We humans are great at devising excuses for ourselves.

I, however, disagree that the Sacrament of Reconciliation

is dead, or even dying. I disagree that it is meaningless for today's Catholics and will soon become a relic of Church history that our grandchildren will only read about.

To paraphrase G.K. Chesterton, it is not that the Sacrament of Reconciliation has been tried and found wanting; it mostly hasn't been tried. And it mostly hasn't been tried because it mostly hasn't been understood.

Reconciliation is best understood as a sacrament that celebrates the reality that human beings *can* grow, change, heal and be healed, forgive and be forgiven, renew themselves and their world, become more whole and blossom into greater beauty. It is offered to all who appreciate the hopefulness that springtime symbolizes: the magnificent mystery that out of seeming death comes new life—not because of anything *we* do but because of God's continuous, uncompromising, unconditional love and initiative.

The Sacrament of Reconciliation is truly a new Rite of Spring through which the Church—and each one of us—can be continually renewed. This book is an attempt to deepen our understanding and appreciation of this sacrament of new life.

CHAPTER ONE

Revising Rites, Renewing People

Throughout history people of all cultures have always had need for rituals celebrating repentance, forgiveness, conversion and reconciliation. Are 20th-century Catholics any different?

Flannery O'Connor, the 20th-century writer, once wrote to a friend: "...the operation of the Church is entirely set up for the sinner, which creates much misunderstanding among the smug" (*The Habit of Being: The Letters of Flannery O'Connor*). Is it possible that those of us who have recently avoided the Sacrament of Reconciliation with a vengeance are "the smug"? Possibly, but I believe that any such smugness will fade as we gain a clearer understanding of sacraments in general and the Sacrament of Reconciliation in particular.

We have revised our rites, now we are in the process of revising ourselves. We must make the effort to understand and appreciate the new Rite of Reconciliation, and the place to begin is with the new sacramental theology on which the Rite is based.

Most of us over 35 grew up with this well-memorized *Baltimore Catechism* definition: "A sacrament is an outward sign instituted by Christ to give grace." It is a fair enough definition; it just doesn't go quite far enough.

Today, with our renewed theology and reformed liturgical rites, we have come to see sacraments in a much broader sense than our catechism definition might suggest. But if we go back to the *origins* of our catechism definition, we can find the origins of our "new" sacramental theology as well.

St. Augustine in the fifth century defined a sacrament as "a visible sign of invisible grace." From Augustine, the phrase filtered down to us through the Middle Ages, the Council of Trent and scholastic theology. Each age elaborated on it and viewed it through its own theological and cultural perspectives. Then in 1884 the Council of Baltimore, which produced the *Baltimore Catechism*, gave us the definition that we grew up with—with its emphasis on the ritual already established.

Our understanding of sacraments today begins not with seven Church rituals, but with people and their experience of God's presence and care in their daily lives. The sacraments are more than ritual acts that give grace; rather, they are opportunities for people already in God's grace to gather and celebrate that fact through symbolic action or ritual.

Sacraments are actions, not things. They are actions of God for people. Sacraments don't happen in Church so much as they happen in people who come together as Church to celebrate what has already been happening in them. Sacraments are lived long before they are celebrated. Or, as St. Augustine put it, they are "visible signs of invisible grace."

Theologians call this incarnational theology, or the incarnational principle. But whether we say it is incarnational theology or sacramental theology, we are saying the same thing: God's way to us and our way to God is in and through the *human*. We are body-persons; there is no other way for us to experience the invisible except through that which we can touch, taste, smell, see, hear, feel. That's why ritual is so important to us: Ritual enables us to enact bodily the belief that God has touched our lives in special ways. Ritual enables us to enact the faith that is within.

In *The Story of My Life* Helen Keller, the courageous woman who was blind and deaf from infancy, tells the story of what she considers the most important day in her life. Her experience says something significant about the capacity of ordinary encounters to become sacramental encounters—visible signs of an invisible reality—if we are open to seeing them that way. On that most important day Helen and her teacher, Anne Sullivan, walked together to the well-house where someone was pumping water. Anne held Helen's hand under the water, and as the cool water gushed over it, Anne spelled the word *water* into the other hand. Helen describes the experience this way:

I stood still, my whole attention fixed upon the motions of her fingers. Suddenly I felt a misty consciousness as of something forgotten—a thrill of returning thought, and somehow the mystery of language was revealed to me. I knew then that "w-a-t-e-r" meant the wonderful cool something that was flowing over my hand. That living word awakened my soul, gave it light, hope, joy, set it free! ...As we returned to the house every object I touched seemed to quiver with life. That was because I saw everything with the strange, new sight that had come to me.

Although she doesn't say so specifically, Helen's experience can be interpreted as a profound experience of God's presence and loving care. The ritual sacraments of the Church originate in the same kind of human, bodily experience of persons of faith. What we ritualize sacramentally is the living human experiences of God we have already had. If the human experience has not happened, then the sacramental ritual makes no sense; it becomes just an empty gesture.

For example, most of us probably have a strong, living sense of God's forgiving and reconciling presence apart from our celebration of the sacrament of forgiveness and reconciliation. We experience that presence of God's forgiveness and reconciliation in our relationships with family and friends every time we forgive, are forgiven and come back together again in loving reconciliation. But when we come together to ritualize God's forgiveness and reconciliation sacramentally, we *realize* and celebrate this living sense of God's love in our lives in a special way.

Similarly, we may have a strong, living sense of God's loving and nourishing presence apart from sharing that presence in the Eucharist. But when we share Christ's Body in the Eucharist, we realize and celebrate that presence in a special way.

Even in the case of infant Baptism, God's love doesn't begin with the celebration of the sacrament. Rather, at the time of Baptism, the Church celebrates the overflowing love that God has had for that child from the time the child began to exist. Thus, in a true sense, the sacraments are signs of what is already happening between God and us 24 hours a day. This reality is what we formally ritualize and make real in a special manner when the sacrament is celebrated liturgically.

Broadening the Notion of Sacrament

To understand how this can be, we must broaden our concept of sacrament and make a distinction between sacraments in general and the Church's seven ritual sacraments. A sacrament in the broadest sense can be any person, event or thing through which we encounter God in a new or deeper way. Such encounters are special moments which can heighten our awareness of God's grace meeting us everywhere.

The psalmist expresses well this notion of human encounter revealing God's presence. Psalm 8 is a good example. It says, in effect, "Lord, when I encounter the works of your hands—sun, moon, stars, people, birds, fish, animals—I encounter the glory of you."

A modern psalmist, 20th-century British poet Gerard Manley Hopkins, also captures this broad sense of sacrament in his poem "God's Grandeur":

> The world is charged with the grandeur of God.
>   It will flame out, like shining from shook foil;
>   It gathers to a greatness, like the ooze of oil
> Crushed. Why do men then now not reck his rod?
> Generations have trod, have trod, have trod;
>   And all is seared with trade; bleared, smeared with
>   toil;
>   And wears man's smudge and shares man's smell:
>   the soil
> Is bare now, nor can foot feel, being shod.
>
> And for all this, nature is never spent;
>   There lives the dearest freshness deep down things;
> And though the last lights off the black West went
>   Oh, morning, at the brown brink eastward,
>   springs—
> Because the Holy Ghost over the bent
>   World broods with warm breast and with ah! bright
>   wings.

A sunset, a period of quiet prayer, a storm, the birth of a child, an intimate conversation with a close friend all have the potential for revealing God to us in new and deeper ways. The phrase *potential for* is important here. Such experiences may not always be sacramental for all people. Some aspects of creation are more "charged" with God than others. And people vary in their capacity to see God in these sacramental manifestations because of their individual backgrounds and experiences. For example, a sunset or a conversation with a close friend is a more poignant sacramental experience for me than a storm or the birth of a child. Storms frighten me, and I have never experienced a birth.

In the same way, someone who has never experienced the joy of forgiveness and reconciliation may not be able to appreciate the Sacrament of Reconciliation. Understanding the relationship between the *human* experience of forgiveness and reconciliation and the *sacramental* celebration of reconciliation is particularly important for parents who want their children to experience the Sacrament. Unless children have experienced reconciliation in the family, they will not be able to appreciate the Sacrament of Reconciliation within the Church family.

This broad concept of sacrament is not new. The Old Testament is full of such sacramental events touching the lives of the Hebrew people long before the Church defined or categorized sacraments. For the Hebrews, Creation, the Flood, the dove returning to Noah carrying an olive branch, the parting of the Red Sea, the miracles of the prophets, all had very sacramental dimensions.

The Exodus event (the escape of the Israelites from slavery in Egypt under the leadership of Moses) was definitely a sacramental experience. In their journey through the desert from slavery to freedom, the Israelites found water from rocks and bread from heaven, and they discovered that Yahweh was indeed loving, powerful and intimately concerned with their welfare. They came to recognize Yahweh in an entirely new way, and their whole history was altered. Their response was to sing, dance, tell and retell the story—not just in words, but in symbols and actions through their Passover ritual.

That is how sacraments work in our lives. They are lived and experienced. Then, because words alone are often not sufficient to relate the power of the experience, people gather

9

together to ritualize the reality—to act out, to celebrate—the meaning of the experience in their lives. In the case of Crossing the Red Sea, the visible sign of God's care occurred when the sea parted and the Israelites managed to get to the other side before they could be recaptured by Pharaoh's army. On the other side, they recognized that the visible sign of the sea parting was, in fact, a sign of the invisible reality of God and God's loving care for them, so they ritualized that realization in song and dance about God's mighty exploits (see Exodus 15:1-21). Ritual is that which enables us to enact what is in the heart when words alone are insufficient.

In the broad sense, then, we can say that a sacramental experience is an encounter with God which somehow changes us. And virtually any human experience can provide us with such an encounter because, for persons of faith, the whole world of experience speaks of God's presence. We can only know the mystery of God's presence through persons, events and objects. We enter into more personal relationship with God in and through our human experiences, encounters and relationships.

In the winter of 1982 an Air Florida jet crashed into the Potomac River. Newspapers and news broadcasts carried the story of one passenger on that flight who certainly spoke to me in a sacramental way. During the rescue operations immediately following the crash this one man kept passing on the life preserver to someone else each time it was thrown to him. Finally, when there was no one else, the rescuers prepared to bring him in, but the man had disappeared beneath the water. I know of one family so touched by this man's "visible sign of invisible grace" that every evening for a week they ritualized their experience by lighting a candle and praying for the "man in the water."

The Church's seven ritual sacraments have their roots in this broad idea of sacraments. The Christian sacraments we know today originated with the human experiences of the followers of Jesus. By experiencing the person of Jesus they encountered God in a new way. Indeed, Jesus was for them the sacrament of God: The visible Jesus revealed to them the hidden reality of God. The disciples' encounter with Jesus changed them, and they shared the story of that transformation not just with words and narratives, but with symbolic actions that could convey better than words the power of their experiences.

10

The early Christians *told* the story of Jesus, but they also *lived* the story. Like Jesus, they went into the waters of Baptism to symbolize their new life. Like him, they broke bread and shared it as a symbol of God's love and care for them and their love and care for each other. They prayed for each other, laid hands on each other, healed and forgave—just as they had seen Jesus do. And as Jesus was the sacrament of God for them, they—the Church—became the sacrament of Jesus for each other: Through their ritual actions, they revealed the ongoing, living presence of Jesus in the world, just as the Church does today when it celebrates the sacraments.

Surprising as it may seem to us, our Church is not alone in its celebration of sacraments. Though other religions may not call them sacraments, all religions have certain objects, actions, places and even persons which are symbolic of some mysterious or sacred reality. Hindus bathe in the Ganges; Moslems pilgrimage to Mecca and face the sacred city when they pray; Jews celebrate Passover; Polynesians and Native Americans have special dances for special occasions; Buddhists abstain from meat; Shakers shake and Quakers sit still.

None of these places, things or actions are revered simply in and of themselves. They point to or symbolize something beyond themselves, something sacred. They are, as theologian Joseph Martos has pointed out, "doors to the sacred." They are all sacraments in the broad sense, because they are visible signs of something invisible, mysterious, sacred and holy. For persons of faith, they are signs of God's presence.

Sacraments as Symbols

Certainly Christian sacraments are signs ("A sacrament is an outward *sign*..."). But our theology of sacraments takes on richer meaning if the sacraments are seen as *symbols*, which means they are even more than "outward signs." A sign carries a single, one-dimensional meaning arbitrarily assigned to it. For example, a stop sign has one simple, informative meaning. Symbols, however, have multiple, several-dimensional meanings, and they convey more than information arbitrarily assigned. Symbols bring us into touch with the familiar and the mysterious simultaneously.

A wedding ring is a symbol with such multilayered meaning. At its most basic level it is a sign that the person wearing it is not single. But its meaning doesn't stop there. It has deeper meaning and special memories for the person wearing it, as well as for the person who gave it. In addition, it bears different meanings and evokes other memories for someone who sees it and, at the same time, its very reality as a neverending circle symbolizes the mystery of love between two people who become symbols for others of the mystery of God's eternal love.

Similarly, the waters of Baptism symbolize washing and cleansing, and the mystery of new life out of death. The bread and wine of Eucharist are symbolic of God's care, nourishment, love and sacrifice for us, as well as of our care, nourishment, love and sacrifice for one another.

The new Rite of Reconciliation has restored a very old and very eloquent symbolic action: the priest extending one or both hands over the penitent's head while praying the prayer of absolution. This gesture reinstates the ancient, intimate custom of laying hands on the head of a penitent to symbolize forgiveness, acceptance, healing, comfort, mercy and a symbolic passing on of the power to forgive others as we have been forgiven.

The symbolic actions at the heart of the Church's sacraments are all expressions of human intimacy—a bath, a meal, an embrace, a laying on of hands, a touch, a rubbing with oil. These actions do for us what words alone, or abstract thought, cannot do. They put the coming of God in our lives into body language. They help us break open and share with one another the common human experiences which reveal God's presence to us.

The sacramental symbols are powerful actions, but they require faith. They don't do anything magically.

For example, extending hands over a penitent's head and saying words of absolution is not a magical gesture which produces instantaneous forgiveness. Rather the symbolic actions of the sacraments bring us into contact with present realities—in this case the reality that we *are* forgiven. But the symbolic actions of the sacraments do not stop there. They also bring us in touch with present realities which give hope for the future and have the power to lead us into that future because of particular faith memories which we carry with us.

Celebrating Past, Present, Future

Each of the seven sacraments expresses three dimensions: past, present and future. These dimensions call us to remember God's action in history, to be aware of God's presence in our lives right now, and to stretch toward that which is holy, sacred and mysterious in God and in ourselves as People of God. When we celebrate sacraments we celebrate each of those dimensions. We celebrate where we have come from, who we are, and what we can become.

The past dimension of a sacrament—that which we remember—consists of the values which Jesus lived: love, forgiveness, self-sacrifice, service. The sacraments are, in fact, opportunities for us to live those values by first of all *remembering* them.

But the sacraments are more than mere reminiscing. The present dimension expresses our awareness of God's action in our lives each and every day; that awareness is what brings us to celebrate the sacraments in the first place.

The future dimension of the sacraments calls us to live what we remember from the past and recognize in our own lives—that is, God's loving care—and act out that love and care for one another.

For example, when we celebrate the Sacrament of Reconciliation, we remember that Jesus was a forgiving person (past dimension). We are aware that God has forgiven us, and we approach the Sacrament as forgiven people wanting to celebrate that fact (present dimension). But the Sacrament calls us beyond the remembering and the celebrating. It calls us to the realization that we, too, must be forgiving people, that we are being challenged by Jesus to forgive again and again (future dimension).

In sacraments, Christians gather to celebrate their belief in God and God's care through liturgical ritual. Liturgical celebration—or ritual—is a community's fullest expression of itself. Through story (Word) and symbolic action, the art called ritual speaks to and of the whole person, the whole community; it makes tangible in symbol, gesture, word and song the past, present and future experience of our relationship with God, with others and with the world.

The sacraments, as we have said, arise out of the story of Jesus' life and actions and, as such, are re-presentations of that life and of those actions. Jesus allowed himself to be baptized; he broke bread and shared it, thus sharing himself. Out of those special *actions* in Jesus' life come our sacraments of Baptism and Eucharist. But the sacraments also flow from the very *meaning* of Jesus' life, from his values and teachings. Jesus raised very basic values and experiences (forgiveness, concern for the sick, marriage, service) to new levels. He transformed ordinary human values into spiritual ones by helping people see God's love made visible through their living and ritualizing of those values.

And so, the seven sacraments as we know them today were not "thought up" by Jesus, exactly as we celebrate them. But they were *instituted* by him (as the old definition states) because, clearly, they come from him. They not only come from his actions, but they also strongly reflect his basic beliefs, values and teachings. When we celebrate sacraments today, we celebrate what Jesus lived and gave special meaning to 2,000 years ago, and what he continues to live and give meaning to today through his Body the Church. As we celebrate the sacraments and live and affirm Jesus' values, we, like his first followers, have the opportunity to encounter him, and through him, God. Jesus is the one great sacrament through which all other sacraments make sense.

Sacraments and Grace

Many of us, I suspect, grew up with the notion that the sacraments provided us with a *thing* called grace which we were somehow lacking. Remember the old milk bottle illustration from catechism days? The "sin" bottle was empty and black, the "grace" bottle full and white. The image made sacraments a divine filling station, and grace some*thing* that God measured and dispensed to us if we prayed, fasted, did good works, kept the commandments and received the sacraments regularly. If we worked hard enough we could get enough grace to have a legitimate claim on our heavenly reward.

But grace is not a *thing*, a quantity that can be measured; it is a quality which defies measurement. Grace is essentially the gift of God's love and presence. It is a relationship between God and us. Our side of the relationship develops gradually, but always in response to a love which is already there.

The gift of God's grace is totally free and ever present. What we do with that gift is ours to choose. As with any gift, the gift of grace is ours to accept or reject. Our recognition that we have accepted God's grace in our lives is what we celebrate in the sacraments.

In word and symbolic action the sacraments proclaim and enable us to express our response to that grace in our lives. The grace does not exist because we celebrate sacraments; we celebrate sacraments because grace exists in us and we have responded to it. Sacraments do not provide, or bring into being, something which is otherwise absent; they celebrate God's grace which is already present long before we recognize or celebrate it. The sacraments, then, are not events by which we are rescued from our sinfulness and transformed into loving people. This happens in our daily lives—and then we gather together to celebrate who we are, what we do and what we might become.

The new sacramental rites are very clear about this. The Rite of Reconciliation, for example, describes sacramental absolution as the "completion of the process of conversion." We used to say, "Go to confession and get forgiveness." The new Rite says, in effect, "Experience the Lord's forgiveness in the community, then go to confession and celebrate the reality of that forgiveness."

Similarly, Baptism does not magically bring God's love into being. Baptism celebrates—and deepens—a family's and a community's experience of that love in the baptized and in themselves. The same is true of Eucharist. Although we are already united to God and to others, our celebration of Eucharist clarifies this relationship even more.

Sacraments are lived before they are celebrated. They are, indeed, the "visible expression of invisible grace" which St. Augustine defined. We celebrate sacraments because we *recognize* the gift of grace in ourselves, not merely to *procure* the gift. And yet, at the same time, we can certainly experience a deepening of God's gift of grace through our celebration of the sacraments if we are open to it.

We used to call that experience of growing in God's grace an increase of grace, but that phrase is actually a misnomer. God's gift of grace is given fully. It is *we* who gradually grow in our realization of its power in us. That is why we say that the sacraments "effect what they signify." Or, to turn a phrase, sacraments effect what they signify provided what they signify is already in effect. The marvelous mystery of God's grace is that, while it is always there awaiting our recognition and ritualization of it in our lives, in that very recognition and celebration, the gift becomes even more present to us.

Because grace is an immeasurable quality, it can only be spoken of in *relational* terms. The new sacramental rites repeatedly speak of how the sacraments effect a deeper "relationship" or greater "conformity" with Christ and also with the Church. This strengthened relationship with Christ in the Church is an important aspect of sacraments which can be lost if we look no further than our catechism definition.

Sacraments and Community

Sacraments do not happen only to the individual. Sacraments can be understood completely only in relation to the Body of Christ which is the Church. This communal dimension of sacraments is essential to our understanding of contemporary sacramental theology. It is out of our understanding of Christ as the Sacrament of God and the Church as the sacrament of Christ that we can understand sacraments as community events.

Sacraments can in no way be understood as private "me and God" affairs. Sacraments happen first to the community, the Church. And when something happens to the Church (to paraphrase St. Paul), it happens to the individual. This is why the new rites insist that the sacraments be celebrated in the Christian assembly, with the community present and actively participating. The sacramental symbols are communal symbols which touch us as members of a community. The richness and effectiveness of the symbolism often depends on our degree of participation and responsiveness.

Sacraments do not—in fact, cannot—stop with ritual celebration. We have to *be* sacrament to the world—*be* that visible expression of God's love and care.

16

Sacraments are extended into the world by people whose sacramental lives shape and reshape themselves, their community and the world. Like the first followers of Jesus, we break bread with and for one another, we pray for each other, we lay hands on one another in love, we heal and forgive. In so doing, we help strengthen the Christian community and offer a model for the building up of the whole human family.

Thus, sacraments neither begin nor end with liturgical celebration. They begin with God's love and care through Christ to us, the Church. They continue with us, the Church, experiencing and celebrating this love and extending it to the world. The grace of the sacraments is the grace of the Church in service to others. And, in a very real sense, they never end so long as we, the Church, continue to live and celebrate the ongoing symbols of God's eternal care for all of us.

This is the heart of sacramental spirituality: Because of God's magnanimous love for us, the gift of grace is always there.

CHAPTER TWO

Our Shared History:
Reconciliation Through the Ages

It is safe to say that if Christopher Columbus in 1492 and the first astronaut to land on the moon in 1969 had each gone to confession before embarking on their respective journeys, they would have celebrated the Sacrament of Reconciliation in pretty much the same way.

The practice and understanding of the sacrament that most of us grew up with originated in the Middle Ages, and remained basically unchanged until 1973. But the Sacrament was not always celebrated that way.

Most people don't realize that there were many changes in the Sacrament of Reconciliation prior to the Middle Ages. In fact, some say that this sacrament has undergone more changes, revisions and reforms than any of the other sacraments. Each change came about as a response to the expressed needs of people at the time. And this is as it should be. Sacraments are the ritual expressions of human experience; when our rituals do not speak to our experiences, they are meaningless and require change.

The new Rite of Reconciliation introduced in 1973 calls us to rediscover the ancient yet ever new journeying of our forebears. We are called not to recover the past, for that is impossible; nor to recreate it for the present, for that is fatuous (besides, the Church has no business dealing in antiques). But knowing and being at home with our past can make the present more intelligible, and the future more hospitable. We need to journey to where the Church has been in order to arrive at where we would like to be today. Because our past is punctuated with constant change, history can help us find comfort in the ever-changing present and even free us to be open to the changes of the future.

History shows us that our new Rite of Reconciliation has come about as part of a natural, recurring cycle that has repeated several times in the nearly 2,000 years the Church has existed. It is a cycle that flows from (a) basic needs, to (b) development of a sacramental form, to (c) legalism, to (d) reform. For example: (a) Christians of a particular era have specific needs for forgiveness and reconciliation. (b) In the spirit of Jesus, they create a sacramental ritual that meets those needs and corresponds to their communal understanding of sin. (c) The ritual and its accompanying theology become hardened into an inflexible legalism which often results in empty, unsacramental rituals that people reject as meaningless. (d) Creative reform occurs to respond to people's new needs for forgiveness and reconciliation.

So let us now trace the Sacrament's historical evolution, beginning at the source: the life of Jesus.

New Testament Times

The Good News of God's compassion for repentant sinners overflows the Christian Scriptures (the New Testament). Forgiveness and reconciliation form the core of Jesus' revelation of God as a loving parent who always takes the initiative in restoring harmony. The life-death-resurrection of Jesus is, in fact, *the* reconciling event for Christians through which God reconciled us and the world through Jesus Christ. In so doing, God took the initiative and gifted us with a permanent opportunity to be always one with God in Christ. The complete act of reconciliation awaits only our response.

Jesus' mission from the beginning was one of forgiveness and reconciliation. He began his public ministry with a call to repentance and conversion (Mark 1:15). He associated and ate with sinners (Matthew 7:24). He forgave repentant sinners (Luke 5:18-26; 7:36-50). He told parables to exemplify God's constant love for sinners (Luke 15). And when asked how often we should forgive one another, he unabashedly announced, "Every time!"

Without doubt, Jesus' mission on earth was to reconcile us with God and with each other. In Hebrew his name means "Yahweh saves," and he gave himself "for the forgiveness of sins." In a broad sense, Jesus *is* a sacrament of divine forgiveness and reconciliation.

In this same broad sense, the early Christian community was a sacrament of reconciliation. They believed that the means of overcoming sin were to be found within the community. Those who acknowledged their sin, confessed to one another and prayed for each other would be forgiven by God (1 John 1:8-10).

Although the New Testament developed a theology of reconciliation and mentioned some penitential disciplines, we do not find a standardized, formal ritual of reconciliation within its pages; nor can we "prove" from Scripture that Jesus intended one. The Scripture text to which Catholic doctrine has appealed to assert the sacramentality and divine origin of the Sacrament of Reconciliation is John 20:22-23:

> "Receive the Holy Spirit. If you forgive men's sins
> they are forgiven them; if you hold them bound, they
> are held bound."

(See also Matthew 16:19 and 18:18).

In and of themselves, these texts do not "prove" that Jesus personally instituted the Sacrament of Reconciliation, nor that he intended to confer the power to forgive sins only on the apostles and their ordained successors. Scripture scholars tell us that we cannot even conclude that these are the actual words of Jesus.

These texts, however, are completely consistent with Jesus' attitude toward sin and forgiveness, and with the preaching of the apostles throughout the New Testament. Since forgiveness is mentioned often in the Acts of the Apostles and in the Epistles, we can presume that it was indeed a value exercised in New Testament Christian communities.

The absence of a standardized format or ritual of reconciliation makes sense in terms of the early Christian community's view of Baptism and Eucharist. Scripture scholars today agree that almost all the texts that speak of conversion and repentance are a call to Baptism. The New Testament Christians believed that sin was buried once and for all in the waters of Baptism. They also expected the Second Coming of Christ at any moment. The possibility of falling into deadly sin after Baptism was virtually impossible in their understanding; therefore, there was no need for re-conversion or a ritual of forgiveness and reconciliation.

The Early Church

The Church of the first three centuries was composed of small Christian communities whose members, for the most part, were baptized as adults. Adults interested in Christianity were invited to join the community on a journey of faith. Those who accepted the invitation became candidates for the sacraments of initiation (Baptism, Confirmation and Eucharist). The candidates were called *catechumens* and entered into a lengthy period of preparation (two or three years) called the *catechumenate*. (Our current Rite of Christian Initiation of Adults is modeled on this early Church practice.)

The catechumenate included ethical and moral formation. Catechumens had to prove, by their life-style and attitude, that they were ready and able to renounce any sin and to enter into a way of life that could cause them persecution and possibly even death. The Church needed to be sure that converts experienced true, radical conversion. There could be no such thing as a halfhearted Christian.

The catechumenate process had its own rites of celebrating reconciliation called the *Scrutinies*. These rites included prayers and exorcisms for the catechumens so that they might be freed of evil and able to avoid it in the future.

Like the New Testament Christians, the Christians of the early Church also believed that sin was buried once and for all in the waters of Baptism — and that the Second Coming of Christ was imminent. But the Second Coming didn't come. And sometimes the early Christians did sin again.

The local Christian communities responded to this fact of recurring sin by encouraging their members to correct one another, confess to one another and pray for each other. Fasting and giving aid to the poor were other means of combating sin and achieving reconciliation. At the same time, the Eucharist provided a ritual of reconciliation, with a general admission of sinfulness at the beginning of the liturgy.

The Church assumed responsibility for caring for, loving, forgiving and welcoming members back when they had strayed. The early Church was very much aware that sin was a community illness and that, therefore, forgiveness and reconciliation were also community efforts.

This early practice of forgiveness of daily faults and reconciliation with the community continued for the first two centuries of the Church's history. There seems to be no record, however, of a prescribed, common, ritual practice of reconciliation. When and how it was done was left to the individual community and local custom.

The Era of Canonical Penance

By the third century, the Church found itself faced with a new set of circumstances. Christians were becoming numerous enough to be a threat to the Empire, and a series of persecutions began.

Although these persecutions were brief and usually local, they were severe enough to cause a number of Christians to renounce their faith. Following the persecutions, repentant Christians would come to the community seeking readmittance to the Table of the Lord from which they had excommunicated themselves by their denial of the faith. The Church began to notice that some Christians were sinning, being forgiven and sinning again.

Fearing that they were perhaps becoming too lenient, the Church began to set legal limits on its forgiveness. They established a practice of reconciliation called *canonical* penance. Canonical penance was for only the most serious or deadly sins, called *crimina*. *Crimina* were categorized as sins against the family (adultery), sins against the community (murder) and sins against the faith (apostasy). The community could still reconcile daily faults repeatedly (through confession to a layperson who would pray with and for the penitent, and help the person change his or her habits and accept God's forgiveness). But the deadly sins required an extended discipline which could be received only once in a lifetime.

The specific disciplines of canonical penance varied from community to community but generally consisted of three stages: confession, penance, absolution. Those who wished to rejoin the community after committing one of the three deadly sins went to the local bishop and confessed their error. In so doing, the penitents officially excommunicated themselves from the community and from the Eucharistic Table. Before they could be readmitted to the ranks of the faithful they had to reform their lives. They entered an Order of Penitents and began a course of extended and stringent disciplinary penances.

In many ways, the Order of Penitents was like the process experienced by converts who joined the Order of Catechumens. It was an extended conversion process through which sinners could recover the meaning of Christian morality and come to experience the forgiveness of God and the community. It was, in a sense, a second but more laborious Baptism preparation; through it the sinner could gain full remission of sin and once again be fully incorporated into the Christian community. Like the catechumens, the penitents were excluded from Eucharistic worship, but they could be present for what we now call the Liturgy of the Word. And like the catechumens, penitents had to wait until the Church felt sure that their conversion was complete and their heart completely released from the stranglehold of sin before they were welcomed back into the community. Once reinstated, there would be no second chance for reconciliation if they sinned seriously again.

Penitents were required to perform works of repentance such as fasting, praying, giving alms to the poor, sleeping less, wearing shirts made of goats' hair to symbolize their separation from the sheep of Christ's flock, wearing chains to symbolize their bondedness to sin. Some had to sprinkle themselves with ashes to symbolize their spiritual death, or refrain from marital relations or renounce involvement in politics or business. The penitents were to demonstrate their sorrow with mournful faces and downcast eyes. In some cases, the penances were so severe that penitents were unable to support themselves or their families. Canonical penance was indeed solemn and rigorous.

Although penances were sometimes severe and penitents were denied the Eucharist, they were not cut off from the reconciling ministry of the community. The worshiping assembly offered special prayers that the spirit of evil might be exorcised (eliminated) from the lives of the penitents. In some cases penitents were given guardians, like baptismal sponsors, who journeyed with them toward full conversion, counseled them and testified to the community when they had reformed their lives and were ready for readmittance. The community also looked after the physical well-being of penitents and sometimes even contributed to their financial needs if they were not able to support themselves or their families.

The period of canonical penance might last a few weeks or several years, depending on local custom. When it was completed, absolution—the final stage of canonical penance—took place. This stage usually occurred at the end of the Lenten season, on Holy Thursday, within a simple liturgical rite. The gathered assembly would offer prayers for the penitents, and then the bishop would impose hands on them as he had done after their Baptism. With this ritual, the Church proclaimed that the penitents had turned from sin and reformed their lives, were forgiven and absolved by God, and were reunited to the community and welcomed once again to the celebration of the Easter sacraments with the whole Church.

Canonical penance reflected the theology of the day: Sin was a community illness, thus forgiveness was a community responsibility. Reconciliation with the Church was the sign that reconciliation with God had already taken place.

Canonical penance was a richly symbolic and impressively stringent process, but it did not last for a number of reasons. First, with changes in secular culture, bishops gradually came to be looked upon as judges, and sin came to be viewed in legal terms—more as breaking of divine or ecclesial law than as a violation of the covenant relationship with God and God's people. Second, the penitential periods became longer and more severe, in an attempt to keep sinners from lapsing back into sin. Public sinners might be required to perform a penance until death—for example, to refrain from sexual relations with their spouse for the rest of their life, or not to engage in business or hold political or ecclesial office ever. And, finally, since canonical penance could be received only once people naturally began postponing the Sacrament until they were near death. The period from 313 to 600 came to be known as the era of "deathbed confession."

But people continued to sin, of course, and to drop out of full communion with the Church. The number of people who took part in the Eucharist declined drastically.

It is not surprising, then, that canonical penance was short-lived. The harshness and length of penances, the possible social stigma that accompanied public penance, and its once-in-a-lifetime practice all contributed to the legalism which eventually led to its demise. By the sixth century the Sacrament no longer held any significance in the lives of the faithful. It was viewed more as a part of one's preparation for death than as part of a Christian's life. New needs were calling for creative reform.

At just this time, a creative reform was developing in the British Isles, and was introduced to the continent by Irish missionary monks.

The Monastic/Celtic Era

Christian life on the Islands centered around monasteries. By and large, by the sixth century, monks were the only Christians who practiced any sort of penitential life. The monks not only performed daily acts of penitence; they had also devised the concept of a "soul friend" or spiritual counselor to whom they could confess their sins, with whom they would pray for repentance and sometimes do common penances, and from whom they would receive direction and assurance of God's mercy and forgiveness.

There were no cities on the Islands. The monks customarily traveled from their monasteries through the countryside preaching forgiveness of sins and celebrating Baptism and Eucharist with the people. But because the distances between the monasteries and the people's rural homes were great, the traveling missionary monks could not always be on hand to bring dying people the Church's assurance of forgiveness.

As a compassionate remedy the monks suggested the penitential process that *they* used: private, repeated confession and continuous works of penance. On one trip, the monks would hear confessions and prescribe penances. On the next trip they would pray with the penitent, asking God's pardon.

26

Since the monks were not bishops, the sign of forgiveness used was a prayer of blessing and forgiveness rather than an imposition of hands.

Notice that the pattern of the Sacrament maintained the three stages of canonical penance: confession, penance and absolution, in that order. This monastic practice of penance came to be known as *tariff* penance, a concept taken over from Celtic secular law in which a penalty was assigned in satisfaction for a crime. The practice gradually became part of the sacramental life of Western Europe as Irish missionary monks journeyed to the Continent.

But change is not easy. Tariff penance caused much consternation among the Church Fathers. After all, it introduced individual, private confession—something unheard of in the sixth-century Church.

The pastoral wisdom of the monks touched genuine needs of God's people for forgiveness, however, and the laity readily adopted the new penitential practice. Individual penitents could confess their sins and receive the absolution of the Church as often as they felt necessary, not just once in a lifetime. The new system was practical, easily accessible, repeatable and certainly more gentle for the penitent.

At the same time, the new practice was not without negative side effects. Reconciliation became a private practice between penitent and confessor, separated from the supportive, prayerful, forgiving and reconciling Christian community. This private approach also shifted the emphasis of the sacrament from penance and the communal celebration of reconciliation to confession, satisfaction for sin and absolution. In addition, the penalties assigned by the monks to accomplish satisfaction for sin varied from place to place and monk to monk; some penances were quite severe.

In an attempt to help make the punishment fit the crime, penitential books ("penitentials") came into being. These manuals were developed as aids or guides for the monks, and as the practice of tariff penance grew, so did the number of penitential books. Typical penances in these manuals included: for murder, compulsory pilgrimage and exile; for adultery, payment of damage to the injured party and total abstinence from intercourse; for thievery, restoration of stolen goods; for gluttony, fasting. Lengthy prayer, vigils, abstaining from food or sleep and giving alms were other penances commonly prescribed by the penitentials. Sometimes the penances were so lengthy that there was no way penitents could accomplish satisfaction for their sins in a single lifetime.

As a result, a system of commutations, or substitute penances, was established whereby shorter and milder penances could be substituted for longer and more severe ones. For example, a year of fasting could be reduced to three days of complete abstinence from food and drink; a year without meat could be commuted to a week of bread and water. Almost any penance could be replaced by the payment of alms to the poor.

Some penitentials even allowed one person to perform another person's penance. Naturally, this led to abuses. One 10th-century record indicates that a wealthy person could accomplish a penance of fasting for seven years by hiring a small army to do it in three days. The system of commuting penances also influenced the rationale behind the selling of indulgences which surfaced in later centuries. In addition, it encouraged the attitude that one could "earn salvation."

As might be expected, this system led to a legalistic attitude toward morality. God came to be seen not as a forgiving parent, but as a king who made commands. Sin was a violation of divine law which required punishment, and penances were the means to satisfy the demands of divine justice. The lists of penances were seen as a code of law and the confessors as judges who weighed the severity of sins and pronounced appropriately severe punishment.

In the 11th century the penitential books were withdrawn from circulation. Gradually, penances became lighter and shorter, often reduced to a few prayers. The less stringent penance meant that the remission of sins, which was once attributed to severe penance, now came to be seen in the ritual of confessing. It was reasoned that admitting one's sins to another human being was, in itself, quite a penance.

Since the priests hearing confessions were also the ones determining the penance, in time they began to grant absolution before the penitent's penance was completed. Eventually, the prayer for forgiveness disappeared from the ritual and the words of absolution were applied not to the completion of the penance but to the confession of sins. The prayer for divine forgiveness prayed by the priest after hearing a penitent's confession ("May

God have mercy on you and forgive you your sins...") became a statement of personal absolution ("*I* absolve you from your sins in the name of the Father, and of the Son, and of the Holy Spirit"). Thus, the pattern of the Sacrament changed from confession, penance and absolution by the Church to confession, absolution by the priest and penance.

While the monastic-Celtic system of reconciliation was meeting the needs of people and becoming common practice from the sixth to the 12th centuries, the law of public, once-only penance remained on the books of Church law. Several Church Councils during those years tried to reinforce canonical penance and abolish private penance, but the efforts did not succeed.

The Theological Shift

The theological shift that occurred from the sixth to the ninth centuries was broader than just a shift in the form and format of the Sacrament of Reconcilation. During those centuries, the community dimension of all the sacraments became essentially nonexistent. Sacraments became the exclusive preserve of the clergy.

The community no longer initiated new members into its ranks. They also lost their participative rights in the Eucharist, which had become a drama in a foreign language watched from afar. Gradually people even stopped receiving Communion at Mass. The entire theology of sacraments was reduced to a single vertical relationship: laity to priest, priest to God, God back to priest, and priest back to laity—and all this in Latin.

The vertical theology also contributed to a changed sense of sin. Sin, like penance, became a purely private affair between God and the individual. Only through the mediation of the priest, who had a direct line to God, could this private matter of sin be rectified.

In 1215 law caught up to theology and the "unofficial" practice of repeated, private confession became the "official, required" law of the Church. The bishops of the Fourth Lateran Council (1215) decreed that all Catholics were required to confess "grave sins" to their pastors annually. Finally, the world's bishops in council, the highest teaching and legislative body of the Church, admitted the disappearance of canonical penance and validated the six-century practice of private confession. And so, by the beginning of the 13th century, the external format of the Sacrament of Reconciliation matched the format most of us remember from our youth.

The Scholastic Period

From the Fourth Lateran Council (1215) to the Council of Trent (1545-1563), the external pattern of private sacramental confession remained virtually unchanged. But theological questions about the inner dynamics of the Sacrament still arose. Scholastic theologians like Peter Abelard (d. 1142), Peter Lombard (d. 1160), Thomas Aquinas (d. 1274) and John Duns Scotus (d. 1308) defined, delineated, discussed and debated the theological implications raised by the practice of the Sacrament: the distinctions between perfect and imperfect contrition, mortal and venial sin, temporal and eternal punishment.

Out of this historical era came a more refined concept of purgatory—a place where unfinished penances (in the days when penances were lengthy) could be completed after death. The Council of Trent defined the existence of purgatory, insisting that souls detained there because of leftover selfishness and egocentricity could be helped by acts of intercession by the faithful.

Also out of this era came a minimalist attitude toward contrition, conversion, penance and reconciliation. More emphasis was placed on absolution, making it the most important element in the Sacrament and that which effected forgiveness.

The scholastic era also saw the recitation of lists of sins including number and kind, assignment of a few formal prayers as penances and reduced demands on the penitent. These practices tended to turn the sacrament into an almost magical formula which had little noticeable effect on the person's moral and spiritual life.

A good example of this mentality manifested itself in the popular attitudes toward indulgences. Theoretically, indulgences were supposed to serve as a substitute or commutation for the penance that a penitent had to perform for confessed sins. But, human nature being what it is, abuses of the practice grew hand-in-hand with greed. Indulgences were sold by bishops to earn ecclesial positions, to recruit warriors for the Crusades or to build basilicas.

A monk by the name of Martin Luther denounced the whole practice of indulgences and attempted to reform the Sacrament of Penance. Contrary to popular opinion, Luther never intended to eliminate the Sacrament. He accepted the sacramentality of Penance, but he saw a danger in the sinner's need to "make satisfaction of sin." To him, this made the works of the penitent more important than faith in God's mercy. Luther, however, was unsuccessful in his push for creative reform: The Sacrament had become too entrenched in legalism. The 16th-century Church itself was clearly established as a juridical and legislative institution, reflecting the culture of its time.

The excessive legalism surrounding the Sacrament of Penance in Luther's time seems constricting to us today. But in fairness to both the Sacrament and this period of history, we have to admit that penance actually had a democratizing effect on society. In Confession, kings and peasants were judged equally before God. This was quite a departure from civil law, where kings who broke laws went unpunished, while peasants were severely punished for the same or similar crimes. The egalitarian approach of Penance defied the conventions of the time, for until the Reformation, Church and state were very interdependent, with shared ideas and patterns of behavior.

During the scholastic era four principal changes occurred in the Sacrament of Penance. First, while the early Church had put emphasis on *reconciliation* with both God and the Church, now the emphasis was placed first on making *satisfaction* for sins. Second, *confession* came to be regarded as having its own power to reconcile the sinner. Third, there was a shift toward *contrition* with the belief that if sinners were truly contrite, they were forgiven even before confessing. As a result, this era also saw the emergence of the question, "Why confess to a priest?" A fourth shift occurred in defense of the role of the priest in the Sacrament: The priest's *absolution* became essential for effecting forgiveness.

The Council of Trent

The Council of Trent reaffirmed the medieval understanding, form and discipline of the Sacrament of Penance established by the Fourth Lateran Council. Sixteenth-century scholars did not have the means to engage in the kind of historical, scriptural and theological research that we have today. As far as the bishops of Trent knew, the Sacrament of Penance in the form of private confession had been a Catholic practice since the Church's foundation.

By Trent the theology of reconciliation had become inseparable from its treatment in Canon Law. In a rather lengthy document containing nine chapters of doctrine and 15 canons (laws), the Council of Trent promulgated the Catholic doctrine and discipline of the Sacrament which remained normative and virtually unchanged for over 400 years; namely, that Catholics were required by law to make a detailed confession of all "grave sins" at least once a year and to receive Communion during the Easter season.

The Council taught that Penance was a sacrament instituted by Christ; that it was distinct from Baptism; that personal contrition, confession of all serious sin in number and kind, and acceptance and completion of a penance in satisfaction for sins were required of the penitent; that absolution was reserved to priests alone; and that the priest had the power of a judge (since the sacrament was a tribunal of sorts) and absolution was a juridical act.

The Council's use of this courtroom metaphor is in many ways unfortunate, but it must be seen in light of the bishops' concern about the Protestant Reformers' new teachings. Many of the canons in the document on the Sacrament were definitive responses to the Reformers, some of whom were suggesting that Reconciliation was not a sacrament. Others were rejecting the power of the priest to forgive sins, suggesting that proclamation of the Word alone was sufficient for the remission of sin.

From Trent to Vatican II

The Tridentine doctrine on the Sacrament of Penance remained the normative Catholic doctrine and practice until the Second

Vatican Council (1962-1965). The form that Trent gave to the Sacrament is basically the same one most of us grew up with. Some minor changes, however, did develop in our understanding and administration of the sacrament between Trent and Vatican II.

Most of these changes were made for the spiritual protection of penitents. In 1567, for example, Pope Pius V ordered that indulgences could no longer be purchased and that Catholics could not be deceived into thinking that they could "buy" their way into heaven.

In 1576 it became mandatory for priests to hear confessions from behind a screen. Thus the confessional box, which had not existed before Trent, became a built-in part of every church. (The privacy of private confession now had its own symbolic "house.") The confessional insured the anonymity of the penitent. Some historians maintain that it was also designed to protect women from being solicited by weak or unscrupulous confessors.

The early 17th century brought the threat of excommunication for priests who revealed sins that were confessed to them. This also reflected the concern for the privacy issue.

Some Church leaders hoped that private confession might become an occasion for personal spiritual counseling for the faithful, but this rarely happened outside convents and monasteries. For most of the laity, confession remained an annual endeavor. It was the usual preparation for Communion, reception of which was legally required once a year.

When Pope Pius X in 1903 urged the frequent reception of Communion, Catholics began going to confession as often as they went to Communion—on the assumption that they had to go to confession each time they wanted to receive Communion. Theologically and canonically this was a mistaken notion, but many of the clergy were not even aware of the error. Those who did recognize it saw no harm in the practice, so it continued.

It was also at this time that children first began going to confession. Prior to the 20th century, children did not receive Eucharist *or* Penance until they were adolescents. But in 1910 Pius X established the age for the first reception of Communion at seven years. And since the practice of confession before Communion had already been established, seven-year-olds were expected to receive the Sacrament of Penance before their First Communion.

In 1943 Pope Pius XI encouraged the practice of frequent confession, and parish priests began providing regular times for the sacrament. Parish bulletins announced: "Confessions will be heard Saturday from 2-5 p.m." And most of us grew up "going to confession" regularly and frequently. The prevalent attitude toward the Sacrament went something like this: "Through the priest who heard our confession, made judgments regarding our sins, and assigned penances to enable us to merit forgiveness, we managed to change God's opinion of us."

This attitude did little to call us to conversion. Our habit of overly frequent confession led to a memorized formula used by every Catholic and to the mechanical recitation of a "grocery list" of trivial matters which often remained the same from confession to confession. Because we saw the confessor as both judge and jury, we tended to search for an "easy" priest who would give a light penance before saying the "magic" words that would once again whiten our sinful souls and assure us of salvation.

In addition, the dark, quiet confessional made the Sacrament not only private, but privatized. It fostered the old understanding of sin as individualistic. With such concentration on self, personal sexual impurity, missing Sunday Mass or private prayers, and eating meat on Friday became the big top three on the hit parade of sins. This privatized, individualistic character of the Sacrament shielded both priest and penitent from the ministry of a forgiving and reconciling community.

Confession was in many ways a dark and private courtroom drama. Sin was a matter of breaking laws. And absolution was an almost magical Latin incantation which we assumed God understood and responded to by infusing us with grace. Thus, for many people the Sacrament was reduced to the level of a rabbit's foot: We believed—somewhat superstitiously—that if we went to confession regularly we could automatically ward off the evil of sin.

Once again, the Sacrament of Reconciliation had become entrenched in legalism. People were deprived of the chance to know the true joy of forgiveness. And once again Christians cried out for creative reform.

Vatican II Reform

Did you begin confessing less frequently in the 1960's and early 1970's (assuming you were old enough, of course)? Most middle-aged Catholics did. Sociologists tell us that the 1950's were a watershed for theological, social and economic values and disciplines in Western civilization. And as the shift in attitudes began to affect Catholics, we began to question the significance of the Sacrament of Penance as we knew it.

As long as sin was understood in legal metaphors, the format of the Sacrament made sense. But in the 60's new theological and philosophical theories suggested that sin had to do with breaking relationships more than breaking rules, with failing to love more than failing to keep laws. Scripture scholarship and study helped us place those theories within a larger perspective. The basic moral teaching of the Bible about sin and reconciliation was not law, we discovered, but covenant—between God and God's people.

The 60's and 70's were also years of social and political unrest and protest. Our renewed understanding of Scripture, theology and psychology shed a different light on our experiences and, in some cases, pricked our consciences. We felt uneasy that in a land of affluence, millions lived in poverty; in a land of freedom for all, some were denied civil rights; in a "civilized" world, innocent people were being slaughtered—by U.S.-made weapons and sometimes by our own military in southeast Asia.

How could people who called themselves Christians allow these things to happen? What did missing Mass, eating meat or the many other aspects of our legalistic morality have to do with these larger issues? In the face of such heinous social sin, what relevance did the practice of private confession with its list of personal sins hold for us as individuals or as Church? The answer many Catholics came up with was, "Seemingly none, so why go?"

In an attempt to respond to these concerns of the laity, pastorally minded parish ministers offered communal penance services. These services gathered an assembly of pray-ers to support one another as they approached the privacy of the confessional to confess their serious sins and receive absolution. The services included Scripture readings, song, common prayer and homilies, often on the social aspects of sin and reconciliation. In many ways they were educational as well as sacramental services, and they seemed to meet the needs of Catholics who were growing in their social awareness of sin, conversion and reconciliation.

At the same time, the bishops of the world were gathering at the Vatican, opening windows and airing out some musty, 400-year-old rules, regulations, teachings and theology. There they heard the Church's plea for reform of the Sacrament of Penance. They also heard from historians that the Sacrament had gone through many changes in the past and could most likely change again in the present. They learned from theologians and scholars of Scripture, philosophy and psychology a deeper understanding of the social dimension of sin and reconciliation. They also learned the limiting effect of viewing sin and the Sacrament of Penance in privatized and legalistic terms.

Although the bishops of Vatican II said nothing specific about the direction that the revision of the Sacrament would take, they did offer some general principles on which reform should be based. In the *Constitution on the Sacred Liturgy* they said simply: "The rite and formulas for the sacrament of penance are to be revised so that they give more luminous expression to both the nature and effect of the sacrament" (#72).

The Dogmatic Constitution on the Church set a clear direction for an understanding of the theology of the Sacrament. There the bishops reiterated a theology that was almost lost in the time since the Council of Trent. "Those who approach the sacrament of penance," they said, "obtain pardon from the mercy of God for offenses committed against Him. They are at the same time reconciled with the Church, which they have wounded by their sins, and which by charity, example, and prayer seeks their conversion" (#11).

The bishops then appointed a liturgical commission to work on the revision of the Sacrament. The result of the commission's study was a new *Rite of Penance* promulgated in 1973, which officially replaced the Tridentine Rite of 1614.

On to a New Era

This 2,000-year history of the Sacrament of Penance is the story of the Church's struggle to be faithful to the needs of the People of God, while at the same time struggling to be faithful to the Good News of redemption and reconciliation. Each chapter in this story reflects the Church's historical situation and its ability to adjust its sacramental practices to the needs of people.

In the course of the story, mercy was meted out, forgiveness found, conversion continued, reconciliation reached and, yes, mistakes made. This is not to say that the shape the Sacrament took in any given era was inauthentic or not a sincere expression of the gospel as it was understood at the time. Each era responded to the spiritual needs of people within the limits of a specific cultural and historical context. Though in hindsight we may label a particular form and theological expression of the Sacrament as limiting, we cannot label it inauthentic for its time. Someday in the future, historians and theologians may consider our new Rite equally limiting for their time.

The Church is a human institution. Its story is our story. It is the human story of us, the People of God, striving to live the Paschal Mystery—the life, death and resurrection of Christ—in our own time and place.

The historical pattern of the Sacrament of Penance—moving from need, to the new form, to legalism, to creative reform will probably not end with the new Rite of Vatican II. At some point the Church once again will refashion the Sacrament of Penance so that it aptly expresses and enhances the People of God's experience of forgiveness and reconciliation.

CHAPTER THREE

New Rite, New Name, New Attitude

The new Rite of Penance emanating from Vatican II is really not one rite but three—one individual, one communal and one a combination of individual and communal elements. Each of the three forms is fully the Sacrament of Penance. Each signifies and effects the forgiveness of sin. Each is intimately related to the Eucharist, which celebrates in the great offering of Christ the redemption and reconciliation begun at Baptism. Each incorporates praise and thanksgiving for the mercy of God. And each is a liturgy—a *public* prayer of the Church.

One Sacrament, Three Forms

The *individual form* is an adaptation of the Tridentine Rite, with emphasis on reconciliation rather than absolution. A prayer for God's mercy now prefaces the words of absolution. The priest and penitent are encouraged to face one another rather than hide on opposite sides of a screen in a dark confessional box.

This new individual form also calls for an atmosphere of prayer and spiritual direction rather than ecclesial judgment. Priest and penitent are encouraged to spend time praying and reflecting on appropriate Scripture passages, and priests are encouraged to assign penances related to the penitent's conversion needs. For this new individual form to be celebrated meaningfully, more time is required than in our recent past.

The *communal form* is reserved for circumstances in which there are large numbers of penitents or insufficient time for individual confessions. The communal Penance service includes hymns, readings from Scripture, a homily or call to reconciliation and prayers of praise and thanks. The gathered assembly is invited to confess their sins to God in their hearts; then the presider prays for God's pardon and absolution over all present.

The new Rite stipulates that, while this form is fully sacramental, those who have committed serious (i.e., mortal) sin must avail themselves of individual confession before taking advantage of communal reconciliation again. This stipulation is in keeping with the Church law that individuals confess serious sin at least once a year. But apart from legal considerations this stipulation reflects a genuine pastoral concern: to provide the penitent an opportunity for personal counseling and spiritual direction within the individual form of the Sacrament.

The *communal/individual form* is actually the Church's way of "officializing" a form of the Sacrament that grew out of the creativity of the laity and their pastoral ministers. This form, like the communal, includes hymns, prayers, readings from Scripture and a homily or call to reconciliation. Then the assembly is invited to approach the minister(s) of the Sacrament for individual confession. Each penitent receives a penance, and the minister prays the prayer of absolution over each one individually. After the individual confessions and absolutions, all pray a final prayer of praise and thanks and are dismissed with a blessing from the presider.

The essence of the new Rite, however, lies not in its various formats, but in its renewed theology—and particularly in our understanding of that theology. In fact, I would propose that the most fundamental change in the new Rite lies in our change of attitude toward the Sacrament. The new Rite offers a wonderfully fresh emphasis in the celebration of forgiveness and reconciliation. That fresh, new emphasis begins with the name we now give to the Sacrament.

What's in a Name?

To my knowledge, William Shakespeare in his play *Romeo and Juliet* was the first person to ask that question:

What's in a name?
That which we call a rose
By any other name would smell as sweet.

Well, that may be true for Shakespeare and for roses, but for this Sacrament that we have called "Penance," "Confession" and now "Reconciliation," the name change is significant. In fact, we might say, the name change makes this rose smell a lot sweeter.

Throughout history, the Sacrament has been called by various names, each of which expresses a particular understanding and attitude.

"Penance," its most ancient name, focuses on the major part of the ritual action as practiced by the early Church: namely, long years of penitential acts designed to effect a change of heart, followed by the joyful return of the penitent to the ranks of the faithful.

"Confession" became the popular name for this Sacrament during the days of the frequent, private ritual. Again the name suggests the emphasis: self-accusation of guilt and confession of all sins by number and kind to a confessor.

Although the new 1973 Rite is officially titled *The Rite of Penance*, calling the Sacrament Penance seems to be confined only to the title. The name "Rite of Reconciliation" rather than "Rite of Penance" is used throughout the document. This recent name change reveals a dramatic holistic development in the Church's understanding, practice and theology of sin, contrition and conversion.

Calling the Sacrament "Reconciliation" emphasizes that its goal is more inclusive than confession, more inclusive than penance, more inclusive even than forgiveness of sins. Surely, that is all part of the Sacrament, but the real goal is *reconciliation*. To reconcile means to bring together that which is apart, to bind, to heal, to make whole again. Thus, the Sacrament of Reconciliation aims at restoring broken relationships, reestablishing lost harmony and peace with people, with creation and, therefore, with God.

The Roots of Reconciliation

"Reconciliation" is the most theologically and scripturally accurate name for the Sacrament. The roots of the Sacrament lie in the Old Testament concept of atonement—being *at one* again with God and one's sisters and brothers. Yom Kippur (Day of Atonement) still is one of the highest Jewish holidays. Jews celebrate it with acknowledgments of sinfulness, penitential practices, acts of contrition, prayers for mercy and a change of heart—all of which are specified conditions for atonement and reconciliation in the Hebrew Scriptures.

In the New Testament, the most radical and central aspect of Jesus' ministry was his work of reconciliation. The Good News he proclaimed is the news of liberation from all that dehumanizes, alienates, oppresses or limits human fulfillment—from all that cuts us off from ourselves, others and God. And Jesus not only preached reconciliation, he embodied it. His very life revealed that God is not an angry judge out to catch us in our sin but a loving and forgiving parent, calling us back and awaiting our return with outstretched arms. (*Kalo*, the Greek word from which our word reconciliation is derived, means just that: "to be called back.") It is important to note that the forgiving parent Jesus reveals always takes the initiative, always does the calling back in reconciliation. This is particularly evident in the Parables of the Lost Sheep (Matthew 18:12-13), the Lost Coin (Luke 15:8-10) and the Prodigal Son (Luke 15:11-32).

When Jesus himself forgives sinners in the Gospels, he does so without accusation, shame or guilt. In the story of the woman caught in adultery, he says, "Nor do I condemn you. You may go. But from now on, avoid this sin" (John 8:11). Even before sinners recognize their sins, Jesus is accepting of them. He doesn't disregard Zacchaeus or the woman at the well; rather, he is compassionate. He doesn't demand that sinners seek or earn forgiveness in order to change God's attitude toward them; rather forgiveness of sin is a gift, and it is God's forgiveness that changes the sinner. The realization of God's constant and overwhelming love reveals to sinners the need to be forgiven. That, as sure as anything, is what happened to Zacchaeus, and when it did salvation came to his home (Luke 19:1-10).

And forgiveness doesn't stop at the sinner's house. Once forgiven, sinners are empowered to extend to others the gift of forgiveness. "Pardon, and you shall be pardoned," Jesus says (Luke 6:37). And he teaches his followers to pray, "forgive us our sins for we too forgive all who do us wrong..." (Luke 11:4). When Peter asks how many times he must forgive, Jesus tells him, "seventy times seven times"—in other words, as often as you must and fully (Matthew 18:21-22).

Reconciliation—A Style of Life

Reconciliation is a demanding vocation. It ultimately cost Jesus his life. And it is our participation in the victory of that reconciling event that we celebrate in the Sacrament. St. Paul explains that Christ's reconciling ministry is entrusted to us, his Body on earth. Through the Church, Christ's mission of reconciliation is extended throughout history. Thus, by virtue of our Baptism we are called to forgive and accept forgiveness, to continue the work of reconciliation, and to the extent that we respond to that call we will become a new creation, contributing to making all things new again.

> ...[I]f anyone is in Christ, he is a new creation. The old order has passed away; now all is new! All this has been done by God, who has reconciled us to himself through Christ and has given us the ministry of reconciliation. I mean that God, in Christ, was reconciling the world to himself, not counting men's transgressions against them, and that he entrusted the message of reconciliation to us. (2 Corinthians 5:17-19)

For Paul, and for us as well, reconciliation is more than what happens at the moment of sacramental celebration. It is a life-style, a mission, a ministry, a lifelong process in which all of us as Church are constantly and intimately involved. Reconciliation sums up and embraces the whole of Christian life. It is the common thread woven throughout the fabric of Christianity.

What's New in the New Rite

The Introduction to the new Rite of Reconciliation stresses this scriptural background and broadened concept of reconciliation, pointing out that reconciliation begins with God's initiative. It is not something we do for ourselves, rather it is something God does for us. God does not reconcile us against our will, of course, nor does reconciliation occur without our cooperation and acceptance of God's love and grace. But reconciliation comes first from God's side. God calls us "from darkness into his marvelous light" (1 Peter 2:9) to be united with Christ and through him with the Creator and the Holy Spirit. This reconciliation initiated by God has the power, if we accept it, to fashion us into a new people who share with Christ a common history, a common journey and a common freedom to move forward into a new way of life.

The new Rite says, in effect, that there is "good news"—even about sin. The good news about sin is that God always forgives, and also that there is now a wonderfully fresh new way to celebrate our experience of that forgiveness. The dominant note in the new Rite of Reconciliation is not fear, sorrow or guilt, but hope, joy and confidence. For many of us who grew up under the tutelage of the *Baltimore Catechism*, this may be the most notable departure from our past attitude toward the Sacrament.

While the new Rite focuses on God's merciful love for us, the post-Tridentine Rite focused on our sinfulness and self-accusation. A bit of catechism trivia may help point this out. The *Baltimore Catechism, No. 2* has 55 questions on the Sacrament of Penance. Of the 55 questions, 45 are concerned with the acts of the penitent in the confessional, or immediately before and after the confession. This emphasis on making a technically "good" confession to rid ourselves of sin overshadows consideration of the sacrament as a manifestation of God's merciful love.

No wonder so many of us grew up with the false and unscriptural notion that we could earn God's love by obeying all the rules, doing all the technically correct things! In reality God loves, chooses and accepts us *before* we love, choose and accept God. In fact, it is God's love and choice of us—God's grace—which enables and empowers us to turn to and re-turn to God. Emphasizing God's love and compassion is a major characteristic of the new Rite.

Another important feature of the new Rite is this: Besides placing the Sacrament within the history of salvation and within the total life and mission of the Church, it focuses on its relation to Baptism and Eucharist. The Sacrament of Reconciliation is not an isolated event in the individual lives of Christians. It is part of our participation in the total Paschal Mystery and the total life of the penitent Church.

In 1983 when the Synod of Bishops discussed reconciliation, they strongly reiterated this understanding. In their papers, discussions and proposals to the Pope, they sought to establish a link between sacramental reconciliation and the Church's mission of fostering reconciliation in the world. "The Church," they said, "as a sacrament of reconciliation to the world has to be an effective sign of God's mercy."

The Sacrament of Reconciliation is but one element in this ministry of reconciliation of which both the bishops and St. Paul speak. For reconciliation is not confined to, but completed by sacramental celebration. The sacramental celebration of reconciliation is a peak moment in the Christian's ongoing journey of conversion. That journey begins at Baptism which initiates us into the life, death and resurrection of Christ (the Paschal Mystery); and it finds its fullness and completion in the Eucharist.

The Eucharist is the primary sacramental sign of Christ's love for sinners. It is, therefore, *the* great Sacrament of Reconciliation. In any celebration of Eucharist—if you pay close attention—you will notice that there are no less than 70 references to forgiveness, mercy and reconciliation. Eucharist is the sacrifice of the new covenant for the forgiveness of sins; it is the Passion of Christ made present and offered again to God by the Church for the salvation of the world.

Participation in Eucharist is seen as the culmination of reconciliation. After describing absolution as God's welcome of the penitent, the Introduction to the new Rite says: "This [absolution] is finally expressed in a renewed and more fervent sharing of the Lord's Table, and there is great joy at the banquet of God's Church over the son who has returned from afar."

We could say that all of this is the Church's way of responding to the very human "passages" in our lives. We are initiated, welcomed and accepted into the Christian community through Baptism, Confirmation and Eucharist. Then, because the community is made up of sinful human beings who sometimes turn in on themselves and in various ways separate themselves from the community and their God, the Church offers the Sacrament of Reconciliation. This Sacrament enables those very human people to renew their initiation with a special ritual celebration and return, reconciled to the community and God.

A Communal Celebration

The phrase *ritual celebration* is important in our renewed understanding and attitude toward the Sacrament of Reconciliation. The phrase denotes that the celebration of the Sacrament is a *liturgy*—that is, a *public* worship service of the Church, not a *private* event between priest and penitent or between penitent and God.

The new Rite reinstates the Christian community as the first ministers of the Sacrament. The Introduction makes this clear when it says:

> The whole Church, as a priestly people, acts in different ways in the work of reconciliation which has been entrusted to it by the Lord. Not only does the Church call sinners to repentance by preaching the word of God, but it also intercedes for them and helps penitents with maternal care and solicitude to acknowledge and admit their sins and so obtain the mercy of God who alone can forgive sins. Furthermore, the Church becomes the instrument of the conversion and absolution of the penitent through the ministry entrusted by Christ to the apostles and their successors. (#8)

The Church exists precisely to proclaim and carry on the reconciling work of Christ in today's world, to be a sign of the reconciling Savior. In order to be that sign, we must abandon the illusion that we are separate, independent selves. The very act of forgiving and reconciling calls for an awareness of relationship with others in community. The entire community of the faithful—all of us—are intimately involved in providing the faith-filled environment that fosters the continuing process of conversion and reconciliation. We are responsible for welcoming the penitent back in the spirit of the forgiving parent. At the same time, each of us is empowered to approach and celebrate the Sacrament because of the ministry and support of the community in which the sacramental encounter takes place.

God's merciful love is always enfleshed in people. Words and rituals alone do not touch us at the heart. People do. G. K. Chesterton put it well when he said that God's Son became human because God knew we could love nothing that we could not put our arms around.

CHAPTER FOUR

The Three C's of Reconciliation

This well-known parable is perhaps the most strikingly powerful illustration of the human process of reconciliation, and of the theology inherent in the new Rite:

A man had two sons. The younger of them said to his father, "Father, give me the share of the estate that is coming to me." So the father divided up the property. Some days later this younger son collected all his belongings and went off to a distant land, where he squandered his money on dissolute living. After he had spent everything, a great famine broke out in that country and he was in dire need. So he attached himself to one of the propertied class of the place, who sent him to his farm to take care of the pigs. He longed to fill his belly with the husks that were fodder for the pigs, but no one made a move to give him anything. Coming to his senses at last, he said: "How many hired hands at my father's place have more than enough to eat, while here I am starving! I will break away and return to my father, and say to him, Father, I have sinned against God and against you; I no longer deserve to be called your son. Treat me like one of your hired hands." With that he set off for his father's house. While he was still a long way off, his father caught sight of him and was deeply moved. He ran out to meet him, threw his arms around his neck, and kissed him. The son said to him, "Father, I have sinned against God and against you; I no longer deserve to be called your son." The father said to his servants: "Quick! bring out the finest robe and put it on him; put a ring on his finger and shoes on his feet. Take the fatted calf and kill it. Let us eat and celebrate, because this son of mine was dead and has come back to life. He was lost and is found." Then the celebration began.

Meanwhile the elder son was out on the land. As he neared the house on his way home, he heard the sound of music and dancing. He called one of the servants and asked him the reason for the dancing and the music. The servant answered, "Your brother is home, and your father has killed the fatted calf because he has him back in good health." The son grew angry at this and would not go in; but his father came out and began to plead with him.

He said to his father in reply: "For years now I have slaved for you. I never disobeyed one of your orders, yet you never gave me so much as a kid goat to celebrate with my friends. Then, when this son of yours returns after having gone through your property with loose women, you kill the fatted calf for him."

"My son," replied the father, "you are with me always, and everything I have is yours. But we had to celebrate and rejoice! This brother of yours was dead, and has come back to life. He was lost and is found." (Luke 15:11-32)

But many of us find it difficult to believe in the story. Something about it doesn't seem right. The father, it appears, never stops loving his son. He welcomes him back instantly—doesn't even wait for him to get to the house. And he isn't at all interested in the young man's confession, only in celebrating.

This is not the way we Catholics have viewed the Sacrament of Reconciliation. Even with the new Rite, most of us tend to view this Sacrament with the attitude of the older son in the story: Forgiveness comes only after you recite your list of sins, agree to suffer a bit for them, do something to make up for your offenses, give some guarantee you won't commit the same sins again, and prove yourself worthy to join the rest of us who haven't been so foolish!

But God really is like the merciful parent in this parable: not out to catch us in our sin but intent on reaching out and hanging on to us in spite of our sin. Reconciliation (and the new Rite is careful to point this out) is not just a matter of getting rid of sin. Nor is its dominant concern what *we*, the penitents, do. The important point is what *God* does in, with and through us.

A Journey Home to God

God's reconciling work in us doesn't happen in an instant. Reconciliation is a process, often a long, sometimes a painful process. The human process of reconciliation which we ritualize in the Sacrament of Reconciliation is a journey that is not confined to, but completed in, sacramental celebration. It is a round-trip journey away from our home with God and back again. This journey home can be summed up in terms of three C's: *conversion*, *confession* and *celebration*—and *in that order*.

In the past the order was different: Receiving the Sacrament meant beginning with a recitation of sins (*confession*). Then we expressed our sorrow with an Act of Contrition, agreed to make some satisfaction for our sins by accepting our penance, and resolved to change our ways (*conversion*). *Celebration* was seldom, if ever, part of the process.

The Parable of the Prodigal Son at the beginning of this chapter can help us understand the stages in our journey to reconciliation—and the order in which they occur. This helps us see why the theology of the new Rite of Reconciliation suggests a reordering in the pattern that we were familiar with in the past.

The journey for the young man in the parable (and for us) begins with the selfishness of sin. His sin takes him from the home of his parents—as our sin takes us from the shelter of God and the Christian community. His major concern in his new self-centered life-style—as is ours in sin—is himself and his personal gratification: fine food for his stomach, fancy clothes for his body and fly-by-night friends for his enjoyment. None of the relationships he establishes in his ego-centered life-style are lasting. When his money runs out, so do his "friends." Eventually he discovers himself alone, mired in the mud of a pigpen, just as he is mired in sin.

Then comes this significant phrase in the story: "Coming to his senses at last...." This is the beginning of the journey back, the beginning of conversion.

Conversion

The conversion process begins with a "coming to one's senses," with a realization that all is not right with our values and style of life. Prompted by a faith response to God's call, conversion initiates a desire for change.

Change is the essence of conversion. *Shuv*, the Old Testament term for conversion, suggests a physical change of direction. The implication is that one has been traveling in the wrong direction and needs to make an "about-face."

Metanoia, the New Testament term for conversion, suggests an internal turnabout, a change of heart that is revealed in one's conduct. As the Introduction to the new Rite says:

> We can only approach the Kingdom of Christ by *metanoia*. This is a profound change of the whole person by which one begins to consider, judge, and arrange [one's] life according to the holiness and love of God, made manifest in his Son in the last days and given to us in abundance. (#6a)
> ...God grants pardon to the sinner who in sacramental confession manifests his change of heart. (#6d)

The Gospel vision of *metanoia* calls for an interior transformation that comes about when God's Spirit breaks into our lives with the Good News that God loves us unconditionally. Conversion is always a response to being loved by God. In fact, the most important part of the conversion process is the experience of being loved and realizing that God's love saves us—we do not save ourselves. Our part in this saving action is to be open to the gift of God's love—to be open to grace. Moral conversion means making a personal, explicitly responsible decision to turn away from the evil that blinds us to God's love, and to turn toward God who gifts us with love in spite of our sinfulness.

Persons who turn to God in conversion will never be the same again, because conversion implies transformation of the way we relate to others, to ourselves, to the world, to the universe and to God. It is what Fredrick Nietzsche called the "transformation of values." Unless we experience that kind of transformation, or transvaluation, there is no way we can even attempt a sincere and contrite confession. Unless we can see that our values, attitudes and actions are in conflict with Christian ones, we will never see a need to change or desire to be reconciled.

While *metanoia* implies a turnaround in one's life, it does not refer only to 180° turns. In other words, the need for conversion does not extend only to those who have made a radical choice for evil. Most often *metanoia* means the small efforts all of us must continually make to respond to the call of God.

So conversion is not a once-in-a-lifetime moment but a continuous, ongoing, lifelong process which brings us ever closer to "the holiness and love of God." Each experience of moral conversion prompts us to turn more and more toward God, because each conversion experience reveals God in a new, brighter light.

I think Flannery O'Connor captured the meaning of conversion well when she wrote to a friend who was considering converting to Catholicism:

> I don't think of conversion as being once and for all
> and that's that. I think once the process is begun and
> continues that you are continually turning inward
> toward God and away from your own egocentricity
> and that you have to see this selfish side of yourself
> in order to turn away from it. I measure God by
> everything that I am not. I begin with that. (*The Habit
> of Being*)

Moral conversion means continually accepting the fact

that our lives will be full of change. A life of ongoing conversion is a life of ongoing self-examination to see how well we are fulfilling our commitment to the love of God and the love of our neighbors as ourselves. When we discover in the examination of our values, attitudes and style of life that we are "missing the mark," we experience the next step in the conversion process—contrition. This step moves us to the next leg of our conversion journey: breaking away from our misdirected actions, leaving them behind and making some resolutions for the future.

Let's look again at our story. The young man takes the first step in the conversion process when he "comes to his senses," overcomes his blindness and sees what he must do. "I will break away and return to my father."

Then notice what happens. Before he ever gets out of the pigpen, he admits his sinfulness. And in this acknowledgment of sin he both expresses contrition and determines his own penance. "I will say to him, 'Father, I have sinned against God and against you....Treat me like one of your hired hands.'"

Only because the young man had begun to experience a change of heart—a *metanoia*, a conversion—was he able to repent, admit his sinfulness and do something that would help him reform his life-style and attitudes. Then, in the contrition or repentance phase of conversion which follows, he is able to let go of the aspects of his life that are no longer life-giving.

So it is with us. Contrition means examining our present relationships, in the light of the Gospel imperative of love, and taking the necessary steps to repair those relationships with others, ourselves and God. The repentance step in the conversion process is what is commonly called "making satisfaction for our sins," or "doing penance."

In the past penance connoted for many people "making up to God" by punishing ourselves for our sins. But true reparation is not punishment. At its root, reparation is repairing or correcting a sinful life-style.

In the past we were told to do penance as temporal punishment for our sins. Now, however, we understand that our real "punishment" is the continuing pattern of sin in our lives and the harmful attitudes and actions it creates in us. The purpose of doing penance is to help us change that pattern. Penance is for growth, not for punishment. This is the attitude expressed in the Rite of Reconciliation:

> True conversion is completed by acts of penance or
> satisfaction for the sins committed, by amendment of
> conduct and also by reparation of injury. The kind
> and extent of the satisfaction should be suited to the
> personal condition of each penitent so that each one
> may restore the order which he disturbed and
> through corresponding remedy be cured of the
> sickness from which he suffered. Therefore, it is
> necessary that the act of penance really be a remedy
> for sin and a help to renewal of life. Thus the penitent,
> "forgetting the things which are behind him"
> (Philippians 3:13), again becomes part of the mystery
> of salvation and turns toward the future. (#6c)

In this light, "doing penance" means taking steps in the
direction of living a changed life; it means making room for
something new. True reconciliation can happen only when the
process of conversion has brought us to our senses, prompting
us to turn around, admit our sinfulness, change our lives and
perform specific actions (penance) which will enable us to renew
our broken relationships.

Lillian Hellman provides a wonderful image of this
process of reconciliation in her explanation of the word
pentimento at the beginning of *Pentimento: A Book of Poraits*:

> Old paint on canvas, as it ages, sometimes becomes
> transparent. When that happens it is possible, in
> some pictures, to see the original lines: a tree will
> show through a woman's dress, a child makes way
> for a dog, a large boat is no longer on an open sea.
> That is called pentimento because the painter
> "repented," changed his mind. Perhaps it would be
> as well to say that the old conception, replaced by the
> later choice, is a way of seeing and then seeing again.

Confession

You have no doubt noticed that confession has not yet even

been mentioned in our discussion of reconciliation. This aspect of the Sacrament which used to receive the greatest emphasis is now seen as just one step in the total process.

Confession of sin can only be sincere if it is preceded by the process of conversion, which includes an interior change of heart, contrition and a firm resolution to reform our lives. In short, confession is actually the external expression of the interior transformation that conversion has brought about in us. It is a much less significant aspect of the Sacrament than we made it out to be in the past.

This does not mean that confession is unimportant—only that it is not the essence of the Sacrament. The Introduction to the Rite puts it this way:

> The sacrament of penance *includes* the confession of sins, which comes from true knowledge of self before God and from contrition for those sins...in the light of God's mercy. (#6b, emphasis added)

Look again at the story with which we began this chapter, and notice what happens. First of all, the father has been waiting and watching. Seeing his son in the distance, he runs out to meet him with an embrace and a kiss. Through one loving gesture, the father forgives the son—and the son hasn't even made his confession yet! When he does, the father, it seems, hardly listens. The confession is not the most important thing here; the important thing is that his son has returned.

The son need not beg for forgiveness, he *has been* forgiven. This is the glorious Good News: God's forgiveness, like God's love, doesn't stop. In this parable, Jesus reveals to us a loving God who, it seems, simply cannot *not* forgive!

Zorba the Greek—that earthy, raucous lover of life created by Nikos Kazantzakis—captures this loving God who cannot not forgive when he says:

> ...I think of God as being exactly like me. Only bigger, stronger, crazier. And immortal, into the bargain. He's sitting on a pile of soft sheepskins, and his hut's the sky....In his right hand he's holding not a knife or a pair of scales—those damned instruments are meant for butchers and grocers—no, he's holding a

large sponge full of water, like a rain-cloud. On his right is Paradise, on his left Hell. Here comes a soul; the poor little thing's quite naked, because it's lost its cloak—its body, I mean—and it's shivering.

…The naked soul throws itself at God's feet. "Mercy!" it cries. "I have sinned." And away it goes reciting its sins. It recites a whole rigmarole and there's no end to it. God thinks this is too much of a good thing. He yawns. "For heaven's sake stop!" he shouts. "I've heard enough of all that!" Flap! Slap! a wipe of the sponge, and he washes out all the sins. "Away with you, clear out, run off to Paradise!" he says to the soul….

Because God, you know, is a great lord, and that's what being a lord means: to forgive!

Our attitude toward the Sacrament of Reconciliation is intimately related to our image of God. We need to believe, really believe that our God, like Zorba's, is not some big bogeyman waiting to trip us up, but a great Lord who is ever ready to reach out in forgiveness. That's what reconciliation is about—reaching out and touching other people with forgiving love. God does not love us only *when* we are good or *because* we are good. God loves all of us all the time!

The God of Jesus Christ is a God of constant forgiving love. This is the only image of God that enables us to get to the true meaning of sin and reconciliation.

The Rite of Reconciliation reflects this image of a God of mercy. Formerly, it was the penitent who began the encounter in confession—"Bless me, Father, for I have sinned"—not unlike the way the sinner of Zorba's imagination approached God, or the way the son in our parable planned to greet his father. But both Zorba's God and the parent in the parable intervened. In the same vein, it is now the confessor who takes the initiative in Reconciliation, reaching out, welcoming the penitent and creating a hospitable environment of acceptance and love before there is any mention of sin. Thus, the sacramental moment of confession—just one of the sacramental moments in the whole Rite—focuses on God's love rather than our sin.

Go back to the opening story once again, and notice that there is no discussion of the young man's sins. His father doesn't moralize on the wrong he did; he doesn't even exhort the son to avoid sin in the future.

Of course the new Rite does concern itself with the confession of sins. But one's *sinfulness* is not always the same as one's *sins*. And, as a sacrament of healing, Reconciliation addresses the disease (sinfulness) rather than the symptoms (sins).

So, the Sacrament calls us to more than prepared speeches or lists of sins (symptoms). We are challenged to search deep into our heart of hearts to discover the struggles, value conflicts and ambiguities (the disease) which cause the sinful acts (the symptoms) to appear.

Such searching can hardly be done in a few prayerful minutes before stepping into the reconciliation room. It calls for deep spiritual discernment on our part—profound knowledge and understanding of God's will and action in our lives. This discernment is a gift of the Spirit which we must be open to receive.

Soul-searching and discernment is not an easy task. But without it, confession becomes nothing more than the recitation of a grocery list of symptoms, and we never even approach the interior change necessary to be healed of our sinfulness. Without an interior healing, and without a firm belief that we are forgiven by God, confession and absolution have no meaning and, indeed, no effect. As the Introduction to the Rite of Penance says, our

> inner examination of heart and the exterior accusation should be made in the light of God's mercy.... The form of absolution (see #46) indicates the reconciliation of the penitent comes from the mercy of the Father; it shows the connection between the reconciliation of the sinner and the paschal mystery of Christ; it stresses the role of the Holy Spirit in the forgiveness of sins; finally, it underlines the ecclesial aspect of the sacrament because reconciliation with God is asked for and given through the ministry of the Church.

Confession is not just a matter of receiving forgiveness but celebrating the fact that we are forgiven.

Some obvious questions arise from this focus on God's love—questions that have been asked by large numbers of Catholics, and that have kept equally large numbers of Catholics from approaching the Sacrament: "So why confess my sins? And why confess to a priest? Why not confess directly to God, since God has already forgiven me anyway?"

From God's point of view, the simple answer is: "There is no reason." But from our point of view, the simple—or not so simple—answer is: "Because we are human beings with human needs."

For one thing, we do not live in our minds alone. It's fine to "confess directly to God" in our minds, but we have bodies and emotions too. As a result, we need to externalize with words, signs and gestures—that is, with bodily signs—what is in our heart and mind. We need to see, hear and feel forgiveness—not just think about it.

Furthermore, as human beings we have a human need to "get things off our chests," to talk things out with other human beings. The value of a ritual like Reconciliation in meeting this human need is argued surprisingly and unexpectedly in Jimmy Breslin's book *How the Good Guys Finally Won*. Breslin suggests that what Richard Nixon needed during the Watergate crisis and his subsequent resignation was something like "the Grace of Confession."

> …with no way to externalize his evil, Nixon had only himself….Keeping his evil internal ruined him….If he had had a method of externalizing his evil he would have had a somewhat better chance against the life he led. It does not cure to externalize, but it provides for a bit more mercy, a little more ability to face the truth.

All of us need help in externalizing what is within, in opening our hearts before the Lord. Focusing on this need puts the confessor in a whole new light and places special demands on this person. Rather than a faceless and impersonal judge, the confessor is called to be a guide in our discernment. Rather than exercising a *vertical* ministry where the confessor is somehow above us, in a superior position, this person is now seen as one who exercises a horizontal ministry, as a fellow sinner who compassionately helps us experience and proclaim the mercy of God in our lives. The ministry of the confessor is a ministry within and on behalf of the Christian community, not over it. The confessor helps to reveal to us the reality of God's love and the joy of returning home.

Another of the confessor's roles is to say the prayer of absolution. Contrary to what we may have thought in the past, this prayer, which completes or seals the penitent's change of heart, is not a prayer asking for forgiveness. It is a prayer signifying God's forgiveness of us and our reconciliation with the Church. The new Rite points out that absolution restores us to the community and commissions the community to enflesh God's presence and reconciliatory actions.

In its discussion of the meaning of absolution, the new Rite does not even mention the priest. The confessor prays the prayer of absolution, not as a judge, or the granter of forgiveness, but in the role of presider of the reconciling community. "Through the sign of absolution God grants pardon to the sinner...(and) receives the repentant son who comes back to him" (Rite of Penance, #6d).

Sometimes I think that the questions of confessing our sins and confessing to a priest are a holdover from our doomsday attitude toward the Sacrament. We have difficulty in ridding ourselves of the idea that we will be interrogated, judged and only then forgiven. But the Introduction to the Rite describes the confessor not as a judge or interrogator but as one who: "fulfills a parental function...reveals the heart of the Father and shows the image of the Good Shepherd." The role of the confessor is to stand side by side with us and, like the father in our parable, to call us to celebrate.

Celebration

Now there's a word we haven't often associated with the Sacrament of Reconciliation. But in Jesus' parable, it is obviously important and imperative. "Quick!" says the father, "let us celebrate." And why? Because a sinner has converted, repented, confessed and returned.

Celebration only makes sense when there is really something to celebrate. We have all had the experience of going to gatherings with all the trappings of a celebration—people, food, drink, balloons, bands—and yet the festivity was a flop for us. For example, attending an office party can be such an empty gathering for the spouse or friend of an employee. If we have no common experience with others at a celebration, we are left with nothing more than the trappings and a devastatingly boring time. Celebration can never be an end in itself; it flows from lived experience or it is meaningless.

I am reminded of the supposedly true story of a man who had been married four times for a total of 25 years. He wanted to celebrate his 25th anniversary with his fourth wife of five years. She refused, and rightly so. Twenty-five years of marriage was not part of their common lived experience, so celebrating a silver wedding anniversary would have been a sham.

The need for celebration to follow common lived experiences is especially true of sacramental celebrations. All of the sacraments are communal celebrations of the lived experience of believing Christians.

I suspect that the reason we find it difficult to associate the idea of celebration with the Sacrament of Reconciliation has much to do with our former narrow, legalistic understanding of the Sacrament. So long as we see the Sacrament as the time and place that we beg pardon for our sins *before* conversion, healing or reconciliation can take place, then, in truth, we have nothing to celebrate yet. If we approach the Sacrament seeking God's mercy, then we are going to have to wait until we experience and relish that mercy before we have something to celebrate with any sincerity and truth.

Perhaps what we need, more than anything else, to help us feel more comfortable with the idea of celebration in relation to Reconciliation is a conversion from our own rugged individualism. Let's face it—there is something about believing in a bogeyman God from whom we have to earn forgiveness that makes us feel good psychologically. It's harder to feel good about a God who loves and forgives us unconditionally— whether we know it or not, want it or not, like it or not. In the face of such love and forgiveness we feel uncomfortable. It creates a pressure within us that makes us feel we should "do something" to deserve such largess—or at least feel a bit guilty.

The older brother in our story expresses this same discomfort. Upon witnessing the festivities, he appeals to fairness and legalism. In a sense, he is hanging on to the courtroom image of the Sacrament of Reconciliation, suggesting that there is no way everyone can feel good about the return of the younger brother until amends have been made—if for no other reason than that the younger brother will be able to regain some self-respect in the household.

But this older son is far too narrow in his understanding of life, of God and of the Sacrament. He is too calculating, too quantitative, not unlike the butchers and grocers that Zorba refers to in his description of God. This son finds it difficult to understand that we are never *not* forgiven. The Sacrament of Reconciliation does not bring about something that was absent. It proclaims and enables us to own God's love and forgiveness that is already present.

The older brother's problem is a universal human one. It's tough for most of us to say, "I'm sorry." It is even tougher to say, "You're forgiven." And it is most difficult of all to say gracefully, "I accept your forgiveness." To be able to do that we must be able to forgive ourselves. That, too, is what we celebrate in the Sacrament of Reconciliation.

And as we do we become more aware of God's unconditional love and mercy. Our acceptance of God's love and mercy is the grace of the Sacrament. It is that grace which brings us to the Sacrament in the first place and leads us beyond the Sacrament as well.

For the Sacrament of Reconciliation is a journey. The moment of sacramental celebration is but a milestone, a peak moment, on that journey. The Rite puts the process in perspective when it says: "Faithful Christians, *as they experience and proclaim the mercy of God in their lives, celebrate*...the liturgy by which the church continually renews itself" (#11, emphasis added).

The community's liturgical celebration of Reconciliation places a frame around the picture of our continual journey from sin to reconciliation. Only someone who has never experienced or reflected on that journey will fail to understand the need and value of celebrating the Sacrament.

The older son in our story may be such a person. When the father calls for a celebration, everyone else in the household responds. Not only do they celebrate the younger son's return, they celebrate their own experience of forgiveness, mercy and reconciliation as well. They, like us, have been on that journey from which the young man has returned. Because of the forgiveness and reconciliation they have experienced, they have been able to forgive themselves and are able to forgive and celebrate with the prodigal.

So there *is* something we can do about the unconditional forgiveness we receive from God: forgive as we have been forgiven. Having been forgiven, we are empowered to forgive ourselves and to forgive one another, heal one another and celebrate the fact that together we have come a step closer to the peace, justice and reconciliation that makes us the heralds of Christ's Kingdom on earth.

Moral theologian Dick Westley in his book *Morality and Its Beyond* says:

> If the only way I feel good about myself is to play some role in earning my own forgiveness, then I shall be unable to enter into the process of forgiveness—reconciliation—solidarity required by the Kingdom. I shall remain too centered on myself to accept the gift graciously or graciously to bestow it on others.

Individuals like the older son effectively cut themselves off from the community. For an important aspect of the Sacrament of Reconciliation, like any celebration, is this awareness: We need other people, and other people need us.

Sacramental celebrations are communal because sacramental theology is horizontal. Sacraments happen in people who are in relationship with each other and with God. In the area of sin, forgiveness and reconciliation this is particularly evident. Our sinfulness disrupts our relationship in community as well as our relationship with God. And since the Sacrament begins with our sinfulness, which affects others, it is only proper that it culminate with a communal expression of love and forgiveness that embodies the love and forgiveness of God.

Our journey to reconciliation is never a journey we make alone; the entire Christian community accompanies us. Because our sinfulness affects the community, the community needs to be involved in reconciliation, in announcing our forgiveness, in aiding us to make new resolves and in helping us to assimilate the grace of the Sacrament into our daily lives. The Christian community breaks open the reconciling Word, nourishes, supports and sustains us; and we do the same for the community. Together we are about the business of making real the ministry of reconciliation.

In his book *What a Modern Catholic Believes About Confession*, theologian Tad Guzie explains the community's celebratory role in the Sacrament in this way:

> The primary function of any Christian community is to be a group of people who accept others and who help them accept themselves, *no matter what they have done*. The world in its best moments wants peace and reconciliation, and every sincere person in the world wants acceptance and pardon. The Christian church is called by God to be explicitly what the world implicitly wants: a community in which mutual acceptance and forgiveness are a reality.

Novelist James Hilton put it another way in *Time and Time Again*. "If you forgive people enough you belong to them, and they to you, whether either person likes it or not—squatter's rights of the heart."

Unconverted "older sons" will always be out of step with the Christian community. Whether we celebrate the Sacrament of Reconciliation with the individual form or the communal form, we celebrate with joy and thanksgiving because the forgiveness of the Christian community and of God has brought us to this moment—and that is worth celebrating. There is no room for the attitude that forgiveness comes "only when you have recited your list of sins, agreed to suffer a bit for them and proven yourself worthy to join the rest of us who haven't been so foolish."

Such "older sons" are looking for what theologian Dietrich Bonhoeffer has called "cheap grace"—grace without discipleship, without the cross, without faith, without Jesus Christ living and incarnate, and without the conversion necessary to live reconciliation within the Christian community. Such a person is hardly ready to celebrate the Sacrament of Reconciliation as it is understood today.

CHAPTER FIVE

Contemporary Portraits of Sin and Morality

All of this talk about reconciliation, forgiveness and mercy presupposes something we've hardly touched on yet—sin. Sin is not, and never has been, a pleasant subject. But to really appreciate and participate fully in the Sacrament of Reconciliation, we need to come to a much clearer understanding of the theology of sin. Some commentators maintain that the major reason people avoid the Sacrament of Reconciliation today is because they have lost a real sense of sin.

At the 1983 Synod of Bishops, Cardinal Joseph Bernardin of Chicago said:

> [The Church] should not dwell too much on sin, as if it were a subject worth contemplating for its own sake. On the other hand, the Church should seek to clarify the reality of sin as a necessary part of the process by which sinful human beings are progressively freed from the bonds of sin through conversion.

Father Eugene Walsh, the popular author and lecturer on liturgy, described the present attitude toward sin very accurately, I think. "When it comes to sin," he said, "we have some badly screwed up ideas."

Our past understanding of sin gave much weight to objective, quantitative factors, often considered apart from people. We mathematized sin, putting it into neat little categories, making it synonymous with law-breaking.

But there are some inherent dangers in thinking of sin this way. First, linking sin only to law makes it much less serious than if we see sin in relation to people who can be hurt and to a loving God. To do what is right or good only because it is a law, or to avoid punishment, is the common moral response of a six-year-old.

Second, legal structures or concepts cannot forgive and restore relationships, while God and people can. When we view sin only in relation to law, or divorce it from personal relationships, we create a false morality whereby we can sin and attain forgiveness without ever once thinking about God or others. Such an attitude turns the Sacrament of Reconciliation into a game of chess in which we maneuver God into forgiving us because we have the correct formula. Third, thinking of sin as an objective unlawful act leads to a negative morality. We avoid certain things, assuming they are bad in themselves. For example, we did not eat meat on Friday because it was the law, and we thought we would be punished somehow if we did. We often gave little or no thought to the importance of penance which was the underlying reason for the law. The sin was not in eating meat; the sin was in refusing penance.

Those are pretty "screwed up ideas." It was this mentality that led Flannery O'Connor to comment in a letter to a friend who said she found Catholics repulsive:

> Catholics are...repulsive [because] they...have a kind of false certainty. They operate by the slide rule...and the poor man's insurance system. It's never hard for them to believe because actually they never think about it. (*The Habit of Being*)

Sin: Violating People

Sin is violating people—not laws. It is breaking or weakening the bond of love we have with God and our sisters and brothers. Rather than something we can quantify and categorize, sin is a qualitative and spiritual reality.

So what is sin? If sin is breaking relationships, then our

sin affects real human beings who love us and whom we love. The least peccadillo *can* be serious and devastating because it is committed against some*one* who loves us rather than some*thing* which may mean little to us. Understanding sin as a personal act toward real people means that we have to deal with the personal.

So the basis for understanding sin is relationships— relationships to ourselves, to others, to nature and to God. Only when we know and understand the reality of God's love can we know and understand what it means to deviate from that love. Only when we truly understand what it means to love our neighbors as God loves us can we know what it means to deviate from those relationships, to sin.

The true nature of sin is a refusal to love—ourselves, others and the Other. Sin is selfishness pure and simple. It is deceitful manipulation of others, even God, for our own self-interest. It is being so turned in on ourselves that we cease to care about or pay attention to anyone else. When that happens we begin to destroy other people and ourselves at the same time. We bring about a condition in our lives and in society that is violent and evil. That is the basic ugliness of sin.

The evil of sin is subtle, seductive, real, corrosive, powerful and, if we are not careful, even unconscious. Ordinarily, sin is not sought for its own sake. It usually begins small and often presents itself as being ultimately good and having immediate gain.

For example, sharing an uncomplimentary story (true or untrue) about a neighbor carries the immediate gain of making us look better than the "poor slob" we're talking about. But such an action is nothing more than slanderous.

Let's look even deeper: This action also reveals that we probably think too little of ourself; otherwise, why would we need to make ourself look better? To the extent that we think less of ourself than we really are, we tend to *be* less than we could be. To be less than we can be is to refuse to respond to God's grace to be the person we are called to be by God and by others in the Church and in human society. And that is sinful. Thus, the simple action of telling an uncomplimentary story may actually be only symptomatic of deeper and more fundamental evil—a person's alienation from his or her true self.

The sins we know and can list are often not the most

damaging. The sin we do not take the time to examine is frequently the cancerous habit that is slowly consuming the vitality of our lives as Christians.

As the 20th-century Spanish philosopher Miguel de Unamuno once said, "To fall into habit is to begin to cease to be." That is the incredible possibility that unexamined sinfulness holds out for us. The real power of sin lies in our failure to examine and struggle against our inclination toward manipulation, domination and self-deceit.

When that happens, we also become blind and deaf to our sinfulness and it becomes easy to make excuses. American theologian John Shea has said that in our failure to look at and turn from our sinfulness, sin and evil gain momentum in our lives and in society. The momentum of sin, he says, carries us inward, away from the concern and care for others—even God—toward our own supremacy. At the same time, sin's momentum carries us backward, away from the future and the promise of God's Kingdom; and God becomes more and more obscure to us. Finally, the momentum of sin carries us deathward, away from the abundant new life that Christ promised each of us.

Sin: Who We Are, Not What We Do

Sinfulness is a state of being, a condition or quality of life intimately related to our values, attitudes and goals. We don't so much commit sins, or fall into sin, as we stand in sin, grow in sin, live in sin.

Individual actions can, obviously, be morally wrong, and people do commit such morally wrong actions. But the more basic issue is our fundamental attitude toward ourselves, others, our world and God.

Yet, some people do very little that is clearly sinful, perhaps because they do very little of anything. Garrison Keillor, host of the popular public radio program *A Prairie Home Companion*, once commented humorously on such sinners in one of his monologues: "Why didn't God use a little omnipotence to make people more interesting sinners?" he said. "Our sinful stories somehow aren't good enough in real life."

Such sinners might find practically nothing to confess in

the Sacrament of Reconciliation; yet they might be fundamentally alienated from God and others through their sin of omission. Just by ignoring people, by refusing to acknowledge their presence, we can destroy them. We are saying, in effect, "You are not worth my time or effort." By such conduct we are killing relationships in the same way that not writing, calling or talking to a friend can kill a relationship. Someone once said that the best way for evil to triumph in the world is for good people to do nothing. Jesus condemned sins of omission as strongly as he condemned sins of commission. "As often as you neglected...one of these least ones, you neglected...me" (Matthew 25:45). Through our sins of omission we allow the hungry to remain hungry, and possibly to die of starvation; the homeless to remain homeless, and possibly to die of exposure; the lonely to remain lonely, and possibly to die of desolation; the innocent to be maimed and killed by weapons and bombs made at our hands.

The "evil" from which we pray for deliverance in the Lord's Prayer is an attitude toward life which either willfully or unconsciously, through commission or omission, blinds us to the power and action of God in our lives. It is against this blindness that the Scriptures warn us to "be on guard...to be watchful."

We begin to sin when we begin to choose self-centeredness, and we become sinful (evil) to the extent that we deliberately continue to turn inward, backward and deathward—to cut ourselves off from others. In the process, we allow evil, the opposite of holiness, to begin to slowly strangle the human potential within us. We gradually choose to give way to a condition which can paralyze, blind and control us. Through such a choice we destroy the bonds of God's covenant of love with us; we destroy the bonds of unity and friendship with others; we destroy the bonds of peace and justice; and we spread fear, hatred and violence.

When sin is understood in terms of relationships rather than laws, all of the distinctions between, and questions about, mortal and venial, serious and less serious seem to be moot. Sin is sin. It is ugly, evil and destructive. Certainly sins committed with malice and forethought are more serious than those not deliberated upon. But the fact is that our sinfulness grows out of a basic attitude we have allowed to develop in our lives.

Our sin is not so much the actions that grow out of that attitude (though those actions surely are sinful), but the fact that we do not try to change the attitude from which our sinful actions proceed. The mortalness of sin, then, exists when people immersed in sin and sinful situations are blind to their condition and blind to the possibility of change for the better. So the fundamental question we need to ask ourselves in terms of sin and sinfulness is not, "What have I done?" but, rather, "What sort of person am I? What kind of person am I becoming? What kind of person can I be?" These are the questions we must ask when we examine our conscience prior to the Sacrament of Reconciliation.

We need to remember that we are created and called by God to be holy, that is, fully human. We become fully human, and therefore holy, when we work to develop our God-given gifts and talents to their fullest potential in service to others. Human persons grow and mature to full human-ness through personal relationships. Personal relationships give us the opportunity to come out of our selfish selves and go out to others. To the extent that we deny ourselves this opportunity through the selfishness of sin, we remain closed and we retard our growth to full personhood. We sin by alienating ourselves from our true selves, from God and from others. At the same time, we damage ourselves and other people by our alienation.

Sin: Never a 'Private' Matter

Understanding sin from the viewpoint of these multiple relationships means that there is no such thing as a private sin. Even our most personal, secret sins somehow cut off the flow of grace in ourselves and others. We are less than we can be because of our sin, and what is lacking in us diminishes Christ's Body. The effects of our sinfulness spread outward like the ripples from a stone thrown into water.

Vatican II expressed the social consequences of sin in its document *On the Church in the Modern World*:

> Pulled by manifold attractions, modern man is
> constantly forced to choose among them and to
> renounce some. Indeed, as a weak and sinful being,

he often does what he would not, and fails to do what he would. Hence he suffers from internal divisions, and from these flow so many and such dread discords in society. (#10)

Christianity is relational. Our sinfulness is isolated neither from the overall pattern of our lives nor the quality of life in the world around us. We have a responsibility to develop a social and global moral consciousness.

This moral call is not easy to respond to. Having the means to live comfortably makes it difficult to keep aware of the fact that the poor, the weak, the outcasts and the hungry have a serious claim to our help and care. Having a good job which supports ourselves and our families makes it difficult to look honestly at whether the institution which employs us exploits others; discriminates according to race, sex or creed; or aids war and militarism by producing weapons or weapon parts. And what is our social responsibility toward the divorced person who stands in the back of church, the unwed pregnant teen, the prisoner on death row, the Jewish couple in our Catholic neighborhood, the people of the Soviet Union?

Father John Shea has said that the real power of sin is found not only in individual sinners but in society and culture, where it grows and gains the reputation of being the traditional and acceptable way things are done. Oh, sure, we contribute to the missions, the Thanksgiving clothing drives and the Christmas food baskets. We boycott the right grapes, lettuce, coffee, soup, cosmetics or whatever.

But the journey toward development of a mature moral conscience (that process of seeing the evil of our ways and of society's ways, and doing something concrete about them), the journey to conversion, repentance, satisfaction and reconciliation is a long and difficult one.

Morality: Heralding the Kingdom

What does it mean to be a mature moral person in today's world? In his novel *Death in the Afternoon*, Ernest Hemingway answered the question simply by saying, "I know only that what is moral is what you feel good after and what is immoral is what you feel bad after." But then he went on to say that he could not always depend on those moral standards because, in the case of the bullfight (around which the novel was framed), he felt fine while it was going on but afterward had ambiguous feelings.

The question of what it means to be a moral person in today's world is not a simple one. Morality is intimately related to justice, a justice that goes far beyond law. Being moral and just, like being sinful, has much more to do with who we are than with what we do. And it is determined by more than good or bad feelings.

The expression of justice and morality in our lives is intimately related to our understanding of the Church. The Church is the whole people of God who struggle to give human life the direction Jesus gave it—upward, forward and toward resurrection—the exact opposite direction of sin. As a community, the Church is called to be a countersign to the situation of sin. The task of the Church is to herald the Kingdom of God, where true human potential can be realized.

The Kingdom of God is the presence of God in the hearts of individuals, in groups and in the world renewing and reconciling all things. The Kingdom is imaged wherever justice, love, truth and peace abide. Signs of God's Kingdom are evident when human dignity, sisterhood and brotherhood, freedom and all the good fruits of nature are a reality in the world. The Kingdom is evident, as Isaiah proclaimed so poetically, when the lamb and the lion can live in the same den—or, put another way, when mortal enemies can live together with mutual love and respect. Then, as the psalmist sings,

> Kindness and truth shall meet;
>   justice and peace shall kiss.
>   Truth shall spring out of the earth,
>   and justice shall look down from heaven.
>   (Psalm 85:11-12)

The justice and fidelity of God—God's covenant relationship with the Israelites recorded in Scripture, revealed in history and proclaimed by the Church—is the model of the justice of the Kingdom. That is the justice to which we are called in our moral lives. The justice of God goes beyond legal enactments, minimalist responses or tailoring punishments to fit crimes. "I tell you, unless your holiness surpasses that of the scribes and Pharisees [the legalists of Jesus' time] you shall not enter the kingdom of God" (Matthew 5:20).

Jesus called for a morality that transcends the strictures of law, convention, arbitration or social custom. In fact, he sometimes acted contrary to the laws of his time when the law was upheld as more important than people. In such cases, Jesus labeled the law as unjust, and not in keeping with the justice of God. Martin Luther King, Jr., translated this attitude of Jesus for today's society when he said in a speech in 1963:

> Any law that uplifts human personality is just; any law that degrades human personality is unjust. An unjust law is a code that a numerical or power majority group compels a minority group to obey but does not make binding on itself.

Dick Westley puts the morality that Jesus called for another way when he says:

> The real moral evil is injustice, because it kills. It kills not only the physical life of people, but it dehumanizes them, killing their political, social, ethical and spiritual lives as well...It destroys human solidarity, affronts the dignity of persons, and is destructive to the Kingdom. (*Morality and Its Beyond*)

The justice of God ultimately *is* God. All that God wills, does and is reveals this justice. God reveals justice through all of creation, which in its original state was honest, true, mutually dependent and ordained for a holy purpose. Throughout history, the human egotistical desire to avoid dependence on God and mutual dependency turned the order and beauty of creation into chaos and injustice. That is the original sin.

But God intervened in history to restore justice. The Exodus event in the Old Testament is a significant expression of the liberating power of the God of justice. And the prophets, who called Israel to task for its injustices, enslavements and exploitation, must be seen as the social consciences of Israel and of ourselves, calling people back to the values of the God of the covenant. (See Isaiah 3:13-15, Isaiah 61, Amos 8:4-6, Amos 5:21-24 .)

The New Testament records God's gift of justice in the person of Jesus, the Just One, who not only lived the justice of God and proclaimed the Kingdom but actually embodied the Kingdom in his own person. Jesus left us a moral imperative: Love God with your whole mind, heart and soul; love your neighbor as yourself; and even love your enemies. Jesus showed us how to do that in his life, death and resurrection. Then he gave us the mandate: Do what I have done so that the justice of God will be remembered and known throughout the world.

In every generation Christians are commissioned through Baptism to serve the Kingdom and its justice as revealed in Jesus. They are the new prophets, the social consciences of their society, the morally mature.

The justice that we, the Church, serve is more than mere human justice, more than obeying and upholding established laws. And the Church is called to respond beyond particular causes or particular injustices, because God's justice is indivisible: The truly moral person must constantly struggle against *all* that is unjust.

For example, a morally mature person cannot promote just causes in ways which are degrading, such as by using abusive rhetoric against those with opposing views. A morally mature person cannot promote life by centering only on the unborn, while neglecting the old, the handicapped, the poor, the imprisoned. A morally mature person cannot use violence in the struggle against violence. A morally mature person cannot be against racism without also being against sexism, individualism, materialism, classism, consumerism and all the other destructive "isms" of our society. And a morally mature person cannot fight one ideology with other ideologies.

The ultimate goal of God's justice is the reconstruction of the *whole* world in Christ. As moral Christians, we work for justice with the vision and conviction of faith, as co-workers with Christ and ministers of his Spirit.

God's justice is accomplished in the world when there is reconciliation rather than arbitration; when people are viewed as more than objects of desire, manipulation and profit; when poverty is confronted not by asking how much the poor deserve, but by asking how much the rich really need — and whether there needs to be rich and poor at all. God's justice is done when the goods of the earth are accessible to all, not as sources of private profit, but as sacraments of divine and human intercommunication.

Our moral response to the justice of God requires that we do good without charge, welcome the stranger without stipulation, share our bread without conditions, care for the afflicted without profiting from their misfortunes, exercise authority without seeking honor, and love and respect even our opponents and enemies without expecting anything in return. The justice of God requires conversion of mind and heart, turning from the societal values which are contrary to the divine value of love revealed in Jesus.

Morality: Relating to God, Others, Creation

The practice of justice and morality is expressed through our relationship with God, with others and with material creation. Those relationships are right, just and moral insofar as they liberate or free each party to be who or what it was created to be.

First, in our relationship with God, we must allow God to be God. God's justice is God's cause—not ours—and the power and the glory are likewise God's. It is God's grace that elevates and enables us to share in the work of justice.

Second, in our relationship with others, we must allow humans to be human. We are not moral and just when we try to do the work of justice as rich to poor, strong to weak, intelligent to ignorant, loved to unloved: That is paternalism, manipulation and exploitation. Rather, we are moral and just when we stand person to person as equals, all led by the same hand of God, all working together to renew the earth and build up the human community in perfect justice and love.

Third, in our relationship with material creation, we must remember that God created the world and saw that it was good. Then God entrusted that world as gift to the human race. The goods of the earth exist to serve the world community. They are to enhance the ongoing development of the human race as signs of the love of the Giver. We subvert God's justice when, instead of using the gifts of creation in common and respectfully, a privileged few use creation for personal possession, exploitation, fear or power.

The moral call to Christians today is to exercise the justice of God so that human injustice will give way to the liberation which was realized in Christ. The moral call to Christians today is to act totally out of principle and conscience, with absolutely no self-interest. The moral call to Christians today is to be moral giants who go beyond keeping the concrete injunctions of the commandments and adopt an attitude of love that pervades all their relationships—with God, neighbor and creation.

We cannot claim to have a mature moral conscience unless we have done our very best to understand God's loving will. The overarching principle for today's Christians is Christ's law of love. St. Augustine's statement, "Love and do what you will," and Mohandas Gandhi's words and actions are examples of the moral magnitude needed in today's world if the Church is to exercise its role in forwarding the redemptive work of Christ for the benefit of all.

People who exercise the justice of God are motivated by an extreme sensitivity to and concern for others. Sidney Carlton in Charles Dickens's *A Tale of Two Cities* is an example. Sidney journeys from being a totally unscrupulous, self-centered person to being a moral giant by the end of the novel when he frees the man loved by the woman he loves and takes his place on the guillotine. His words as he climbs the steps to his death have long been remembered and quoted. "It is a far, far better thing I do, than I have ever done."

St. Thomas More is another example of a man who lived the justice of God in spite of the dictates of social pressure. Thomas is imprisoned for refusing to go along with King Henry VIII's plan to divorce Catherine and marry Anne Boleyn. Margaret, Thomas's daughter, wants him to sacrifice his moral principles. "But in reason!" she says in the words of Robert Bolt's *A Man for All Seasons*. "Haven't you done as much as God can reasonably want?" And Thomas replies, "Well...finally...it isn't a matter of reason. Finally it's a matter of love."

We also are called to be moral giants motivated by love. With love as the propelling and guiding force in our lives, we will continually seek and extend forgiveness within the community. For finally, it isn't a matter of reason or feeling or law. Finally it is "a matter of love."

CHAPTER SIX

Reconciliation and Us

David was nine years old. He had not yet experienced the individual form of the Rite of Reconciliation, but he had celebrated the communal form with his family. One day his parents asked him what he thought the individual form of the Sacrament might be like. "Well," he said, screwing up his face, "I guess the priest and I'd probably talk about how we're getting along in our lives. I'd tell him about me, and then I'd ask, 'How's everything with you?' We'd probably tell each other we were pretty swell guys and maybe go out for a beer."

When David's mother told me this story, she said, "I think he's more ready for the new Rite than I am." I agree with her. But, of course, David didn't have any previous attitudes to overcome or habits to break. Still, we might take a serious look at David's description in light of our own celebration of the individual form of the Sacrament.

First of all, notice his comfort with the Sacrament. This is an important consideration for both penitent and confessor. Although the new Rite assigns the confessor the responsibility to establish a sense of welcome and hospitality, we too participate in the establishment of a comfortable environment when we approach the Sacrament as the unique individual that we are. One of the important new characteristics of the Sacrament is the opportunity to express ourselves in our own personal language rather than in someone else's prefabricated "Bless me, Father, for I have sinned..." formula.

Second, one cannot help but notice that David's concern is not with specific sins, but with "how we're getting along in our lives." The "sin list" approach, as we have said, is not necessarily the best way to get to the revelation of our sinfulness. In the Sacrament of Reconciliation we call upon another person to help us search our heart more deeply in open and honest dialogue. This facilitates a sacramental encounter—when the Spirit reveals more clearly what we are and might become.

Third, David concludes his description on a very positive note. One might, in fact, call it celebratory. More than anything, the renewed emphasis of this Sacrament is on acceptance and affirmation. As we examine our life and life-style we inevitably see negatives; but the joy that comes from struggling with and overcoming the distasteful aspects of our lives is what is revealed in Reconciliation. We are a people sent out to proclaim the Good News. And that "news" will never seem "good" if we do not see its goodness in us, its announcers.

Using the Individual Form

While David's description offers a general approach to the individual form of the Sacrament, the Rite offers a more specific format and structure:

1) The priest welcomes and greets the penitent.

2) The priest prays a prayer that both he and the penitent will be open to God's grace.

3) The priest or penitent reads a short passage from the Scriptures.

4) The penitent confesses his or her sinfulness. The priest may help the penitent make a complete confession by offering suitable counsel and encouragement.

5) The priest asks the penitent to accept and perform a suitable act of satisfaction (penance) as a sign of willingness to begin living a new way.

6) The priest invites the penitent to pray a prayer of contrition or sorrow.

7) The priest prays the reconciling prayer of absolution.

8) The penitent prays a prayer of thanks and praise for God's mercy and forgiveness.

9) The priest dismisses the penitent in the peace of Christ and of the Church.

10) The penitent continues his or her conversion and expresses it by a life-style renewed according to the love of God revealed in the Gospel.

Father Leonard Foley, O.F.M., in the *Catholic Update* "Confessing Face-to-Face," has developed an example of how this format for the new Rite might be enfleshed in an ordinary situation. "The 'success' of the sacrament," he says, "will be determined by the seriousness with which we approach it." He suggests, as does the Rite, that both priest and penitent prepare themselves by prayer—the priest to be open to the Spirit's enlightenment and charity, the penitent to be able to see his or her life in relation to the example of the Gospel and to be open to God's forgiving love.

Welcome
Priest: Good afternoon. I'm glad to meet you.

Penitent: Good afternoon, Father. I'm a little nervous about this, since I've never gone to confession this way before.

Priest: There's no need to worry. We'll just follow a simple routine. The main thing we want to remember is that we're in God's presence and that this is a special time of forgiveness and grace. Let's begin, then, by making the Sign of the Cross together and taking the words very seriously.

Priest and Penitent (slowly): In the name of the Father, and of the Son, and of the Holy Spirit. Amen.

Prayer
Priest: I'd like to pray now that we may both be open to what God is offering us in this sacrament. If you wish to pray in your own words too, fine. Otherwise we'll just pray in silence for a little while.

Priest: Loving Father, you are with us. We trust in your graciousness and mercy and we beg you to open our minds and hearts to your truth and love. Give us both the grace to be humble and honest, to face the reality of sin and also the mystery of your infinite love.

Perhaps, after a few moments of silence, the penitent may be moved to say something like: Dear Lord, help me to make a good confession, to be truly sorry, and to be willing to let you change my life.

Hearing God's Word

Priest: In this new Rite the Church asks us to listen first to the Word of God. It is God who brings you here and calls you personally to deepen your conversion from sin and your turning to him. So we listen now to God speaking personally and seriously to us.

There are dozens of options as to what Scripture may be read—very brief or long passages. Either penitent or priest may do the reading. One example is Luke 15:1-7.

Priest or Penitent: "The tax collectors and sinners were all gathering around to hear him, at which the Pharisees and the scribes murmured, 'This man welcomes sinners and eats with them.' Then he addressed this parable to them: 'Who among you, if he has 100 sheep and loses one of them, does not leave the 99 in the wasteland and follow the lost one until he finds it? And when he finds it, he puts it on his shoulders in jubilation. Once arrived home, he invites friends and neighbors in and says to them, "Rejoice with me because I have found my lost sheep." I tell you, there will likewise be more joy in heaven over one repentant sinner than over 99 righteous people who have no need to repent.'"

Priest: Let's just think about this call of God to us for a few minutes.

Silence. Or, possibly, some spontaneous prayer by priest and/or penitent.

Confession of Sin

Penitent: Father, it's been about three months since my last confession. I am married and have three children. I guess my worst sin is the way I treat my husband and children. We have a fairly good relationship, but I do let myself get into moods when I just withdraw into myself. I resent the work I have to do. I feel my husband could do more and the kids could be less demanding. So sometimes I feel sorry for myself, and I let things slide.

Priest: It's good that you are able to admit this.

Penitent: I realize that it's more than half my fault, and I want to do something about it.

Priest: It affects your whole life when you let yourself feel this way?

Penitent: Yes, I don't pray well, or really love my husband as I want to, or my children.

Priest: Is this a long-standing fault?

Penitent: I'm beginning to see that I had something of this before I was married, when I was at home. I tended to pout when things didn't go right, and to sort of wallow in self-pity.

Priest: What do you think is at the bottom of it?

Penitent: I really don't know. In general I have a fairly happy life, except for this attitude that I nourish and really don't do much about. I'm sorry for what it does to me and to my husband and children. I know God is calling me to rise above it.

Priest: The best thing I can tell you, on a human level, is to keep trying to discover what lies beneath this sinfulness. Maybe you're too insecure, or you need more than normal encouragement. Maybe you're too sensitive, or want too much attention. Don't analyze yourself to death, but look beneath the surface and try gradually to know yourself better.

But the main thing we have to remember is that God is calling you to be more completely possessed by the Spirit. Any sin, all sinfulness spoils God's plan for us. It takes something away from our love of God and others. It makes us less able to do the one thing we are called to do—be perfectly open to God's coming, completely possessed by the Spirit.

Now, as a penance, is there any one thing you feel would be helpful in overcoming this attitude?

Penitent: I really couldn't say, Father. I know it's a long process.

Priest: Well, suppose that every morning this week you get down on your knees and, whatever other prayers you say, you look ahead to something that's liable to happen to you that day. Ask the Father to help you at that moment, to fill you with his strength—so that you can reject being resentful and over-sorry for yourself. O.K.?

Penitent: Fine, Father. I'll do that.

Expression of Sorrow

Priest: Now, in a special way, as an outward sign of your

desire to be forgiven and healed by God, please express your sorrow for your sinfulness.

The penitent may say the familiar Act of Contrition, or use one of the several prayers on the card available in the reconciliation room, or use his or her own words.

Penitent: God our Father, I thank you for letting me see my sinfulness and giving me the power to admit it. I put myself into your hands. I am sorry for the harm I have done to your love within me and for spoiling my love for my husband and my children. I know what you are calling me to. I am determined to let your Spirit possess my mind and my heart and my weakness, so that I can follow Jesus as you want me to. Amen.

Absolution

Priest: God blesses you for what he has been able to do in you. And now, through Jesus, through the Body of Jesus which I have been called to represent visibly to you, God gives you the infallible sign of his forgiveness.

The priest extends his hands over the penitent's head and says:

God, the Father of mercies,
through the death and resurrection of his Son
has reconciled the world to himself
and sent the Holy Spirit among us
for the forgiveness of sins;
through the ministry of the Church
may God give you pardon and peace,
and I absolve you from your sins
in the name of the Father, and of the Son,
and of the Holy Spirit.

Penitent: Amen.

Proclamation of Praise of God

Priest: God has blessed you. Now show your gratitude for his mercy by a prayer of thanks and praise. Please answer "Your mercy is forever" to each of the short prayers I say:

Priest: God our Father, we give you our hearts.
Penitent: Your mercy is forever.
Priest: Son of God, Jesus our Brother, we praise your name.

Penitent: Your mercy is forever.

Priest: Spirit of God, possess us with your power.

Penitent: Your mercy is forever.

Priest: The Lord has freed you from your sins. Go in peace.

Penitent: Thank you, Father. This has been very good for me. I think I see a little better what it's all about. I'll see you again. Good-bye.

Priest: Good-bye. God bless you.

The above sample closely follows the structural outline in the Rite. Notice that in both the step-by-step description of the format of the Sacrament and in the imaginary sample, the priest bears much responsibility. The primary role of the presider is to be hospitable and establish a warm sense of welcome and acceptance for penitents. This is done as representative of the hospitable, accepting and healing Christian community and of God. The presider is expected to show, in unmistakable signs, that penitents are loved, welcomed, forgiven and affirmed in their journey toward conversion.

This new role for presiders is a far cry from the former one—as a faceless, impersonal dispenser-of-forgiveness. Most priests welcome the opportunity to exercise this ministry of compassion. As Father Eugene Walsh says in *Adult Discussion of Sin and Reconciliation*,

> I had no trouble giving up the former role of judge. I find the new role of fellow sinner and compassionate minister marvelously and beautifully overwhelming and infinitely healing.

The presider also has the responsibility of aiding penitents as they search out the deeper reasons behind their sinfulness, and of helping them accept what they discover. This may sometimes mean offering encouragement for continued conversion. And, always, the presider must help penitents see and accept the positive and growthful aspects of their lives; otherwise, the sacrament could easily revert to a negative self-accusing experience.

Making the Most of the Sacrament

The total responsibility in the Sacrament of Reconciliation does not rest, however, on the shoulders of the presider. Obviously, penitents have a responsibility to prepare for the Sacrament honestly, thoughtfully and prayerfully. They may also take responsibility for the time they will celebrate the Sacrament by taking the initiative for arranging an appointment with a confessor. This can afford both penitent and presider more time and leisure for the Sacrament.

The expression of hospitality is an aspect of the sacrament in which penitents can participate, too. After all, it is rather difficult for an open, accepting host to welcome a reluctant guest. Penitents can also assume the responsibility of choosing a Scripture passage that is special to them and their journey to reconciliation. This can make one's individual celebration of Reconciliation more personal and meaningful.

Another way penitents can make their celebration of Reconciliation more personal is to formulate in advance an appropriate penance that addresses the root of their sinfulness and that will further the process of conversion in them.

Every individual celebration of the Sacrament is unique, because every penitent is unique. Realizing this, the Rite allows for modification, encouraging us "to adapt the rite to the concrete circumstances of the penitents" (#40).

An 80-year-old Sister in my religious community reminded me of this important aspect of the Sacrament. After I told her I was writing this book, she said emphatically: "Dearie, that's a much needed book. But I hope you're going to tell folks that confessors are only as good as we make them. Now, I've learned to go in and just tell the priest what I want to do—right off—and that works much better for both of us."

The Rite offers some specific suggestions for adaptation. It says, for example, that some parts of the Rite may, for pastoral reasons, be enlarged upon or omitted. It also notes that a place more suitable than a reconciliation room may be chosen as a location, "so that the entire celebration may be rich and fruitful" (#40). This change may be particularly appropriate if the reconciliation room in a parish is less than inviting, pleasant and comfortable. If at all possible, however, care should be taken to provide a reconciliation room with space, lots of light, color, windows, plants, and pleasant and comfortable furniture. Dark, empty rooms are not much more hospitable than dark, empty confessionals.

The Rite also encourages special adaptations for the elderly, the sick and shut-ins. In addition, choosing Scripture texts and prayers other than those suggested is permitted. Only "the essential structure and the entire form of absolution must be kept"—if the penitent desires absolution. It is no longer given automatically, and penitents may be asked if they would like or are ready for the absolution of the Church. In some cases, for example, penitents may want to return for absolution after working at their new way of life for a while.

Shared Responsibility: A Sample Confession

The following is an example of how the Sacrament of Reconciliation might proceed when adapted through shared responsibility between penitent and presider:

Preparation
The penitent, who has experienced conversion and prepared for the sacrament with prayerful and thoughtful examination, calls a confessor for an appointment. The presider also prepares for the Sacrament with prayer and reflection.

Welcome
Penitent and presider meet at an agreed upon place and greet each other warmly.

Presider: The Spirit of God is here with us. Let us begin this liturgical prayer as we begin all prayer in our tradition: In the name of the Father, and of the Son, and of the Holy Spirit. Amen.

Hearing God's Word
Penitent: A few Sundays ago at Mass, the Gospel reading struck me squarely between the eyes, and I realized that I had to change my ways. May we pray that Gospel together right now?

Presider: Of course.

Penitent: "The tax collectors and sinners were all gathering around to hear him, at which the Pharisees and the scribes murmured, 'This man welcomes sinners and eats with them. Then he addressed this parable to them: 'Who among you, if he has 100 sheep and loses one of them, does not leave the 99 in the wasteland and follow the lost one until he finds it? And when he finds it, he puts it on his shoulders in jubilation. Once arrived home, he invites friends and neighbors in and says to them, "Rejoice with me because I have found my lost sheep." I tell you, there will likewise be more joy in heaven over one repentant sinner than over 99 righteous people who have no need to repent.'" (Luke 15:1-7)

That last line really hit me. After hearing it, I realized that I was one of those righteous people. In fact, I thought I was so righteous, I haven't even used this Sacrament for over a year.

As you know, I am a middle manager for a large corporation here in town that produces hi-tech equipment. I have more than 45 people in my department who are answerable to me. I've always tried to be fair, honest and a hard worker. In fact, I work so hard that my job has become my life, and I have found myself becoming alienated from my family. My preoccupation with my work has caused real dissension in my family because I bring my work home and, as a result, I don't really communicate with my family. I can't tell you when I last had a good talk with my kids or my wife. I don't really listen to them either. When they tell me they have informed me about something, I respond angrily and authoritatively that they haven't. I've noticed that they are all pulling away from me, leaving me alone—probably to avoid my outbursts—although the excuse they give is always, "Dad has work to do. Leave him alone."

And it's not just at home. At work I think I sometimes expect people to work as hard as I do. And, of course, they don't complain—they don't want to lose their jobs. They work hard and, for all I know, I'm causing the same situation in other families that I've caused in mine because of the expectations I've placed on my workers.

Well, let me tell you, there's going to be a change. Starting Monday, no more work is going home. What doesn't get done at the office will have to wait, and my workers are going to be told the same thing. I'm going to be more involved with the family. When I'm home all my attention is going to be given to them. I'm going to start doing things with my kids again, and my wife is going to get a lot more attention and help from me too.

Presider: That sounds like a great resolution. Have you told your family about it yet?

Penitent: I thought I'd just surprise them with the news after I leave here. They probably think I went back to the office.

Presider: You have begun an important conversion and have made a wonderful resolution, but, you know, it may take a while for all of you to rebuild the relationships that you once had. It's going to take hard work. Are you ready for that?

Penitent: I know what you mean, and I'm going to work as hard at this as I've worked at my job. Will you pray with me right now for the strength I will need?

Presider: Certainly.

Expression of Sorrow and Prayer for Strength

Penitent: Lord God, I am sorry for the wounds and the hurt I've caused in my family. I'm sorry for being more preoccupied with things than with the people who are most important to me. I'm sorry for having offended you and my family. Please give me the strength and the courage to begin again, to learn to listen again, to share myself more with my family. Amen.

Presider: God, you are a loving Shepherd who has searched the heart of (*name*) and brought him home to you and to his family. Stay with him now in his new resolve. Grace him with the courage and strength to begin again. With you we rejoice at his return and promise to stand by him as he journeys back to you and his family. We make this prayer in the name of Jesus, your Son and our Good Shepherd. Amen.

God has blessed you in a special way. I just want you to know that I will be here if you ever want to talk about how things are going with your new way of life.

Penitent: Thank you; I'd like that.

Presider: Feel free to call any time.

Absolution

Presider: Now, would you like to receive the absolution of the Church?

Penitent: Yes, I would.

Presider (placing both hands on the penitent's head):

God, the Father of mercies,
through the death and resurrection of his Son
has reconciled the world to himself
and sent the Holy Spirit among us
for the forgiveness of sins;
through the ministry of the Church
may God give you pardon and peace,
and I absolve you from your sins
in the name of the Father, and of the Son,
and of the Holy Spirit.

Penitent: Amen.

Proclamation of Praise and Thanks
Presider: The peace of Christ is with you, *(name). (They exchange an embrace of peace.)*
Penitent: Thank you. I can hardly wait to get home and tell my family about this. In fact, I think I'll stop on my way home and pick up some steaks. I haven't grilled steaks with my family in ages. Tonight we're going to start getting to know one another again.
Thank you, Lord, for the grace of this Sacrament.
Presider: Amen.

In this imaginary example, the presider and penitent seem to know one another. Many people prefer to have a regular confessor. In that way, they can work together toward the penitent's continued conversion. This may mean we might have to put some time and effort into finding a confessor with whom we can journey comfortably, and who can offer us the compassion, encouragement and challenge we need. But it is certainly worth the trouble for our spiritual growth and development.

Reconciliation and the Family

Both of the above samples of the celebration of individual Reconciliation involved the penitents' families. Families are the first and most important reconciling community. Children learn the abstract reality of reconciliation by the way their parents live that reality. And before we can demonstrate to our children what reconciliation is, we have to know what it means to us. It does little good to tell our children to be forgiving and reconciling if they never see us asking for and accepting forgiveness.

In her book *Traits of a Healthy Family*, Dolores Curran lists "a pattern of reconciliation" as one of the hallmarks of a communicating family—the number one trait of healthy families. How well a family expresses or ritualizes its reconciliation depends on how well the family communicates with one another.

Every family has fights and disagreements. This is essential for good family health; it helps get things out in the open. The important thing is for families to come back together again. If they can't, then the sacramental celebration of reconciliation will have little or no meaning.

All families seem to have specific patterns of behavior which say, "We're back together again. All is forgiven and forgotten." In some families, the sign is that someone makes a cake or popcorn and invites everyone to share. "We all come out of our rooms," is the gesture in other families. In a family in which one member takes longer than the rest to get over the pouting stage, the ritual experience in the family might be that "Sam finally smiles and says, 'Okay.'"

Of course before whole families can be reconciling families, spouses must set the example. Many parents I know are careful to show their children that they never go to bed angry. One five-year-old once told me that she knew her parents made up after arguments because, one night after they had had one, she sneaked downstairs and found them kissing in front of the fireplace. That was proof enough for her that all was fine. If this child had experienced a day of cold silence instead of signs of affection before a fire, she would have an entirely different image of reconciliation.

Family reconciliation also means that grievances are not repeatedly brought up. Reconciliation means letting go of past hurts. They cannot be used and reused the way Erma Bombeck claims she uses "Why did your mother wear black at our wedding?" to win arguments with her husband.

Dolores Curran relates a beautiful reconciliation ritual that she found among families in Hawaii. It is worth thinking about:

...the wronged person [drew] a picture or symbol of

the wrong in the sand. Then the clan invited the person who inflicted the wrong to step forward and ask forgiveness and promise redress. When that was completed, the wronged member wiped the symbol out of the sand. Once that symbol was gone, so was the memory of it, and the family or clan stood together again with no ongoing feuds to destroy their clanship. They were whole again, a family.

The sacramental celebration of reconciliation is not isolated from the family's celebration of reconciliation. The Sacrament only has meaning if it is supported by ordinary, everyday experiences of love, forgiveness and reconciliation. If the Sacrament of Reconciliation is to be understood and appreciated, the human pattern of reconciliation must be experienced and understood by individuals, families and especially children. This pattern includes three steps.

Basic to an understanding of forgiveness and reconciliation is the experience of *loving and being loved*. This is the first step. We and our children need to know that we are loved, that others value us. Only when we have been loved by other human persons can we understand that we are loved by God.

The second step is the experience of *forgiving and being forgiven*. After we offend others and feel sorry for our misdeeds, it's important to know that they take us back into their good graces. This generosity of spirit helps to empower us to forgive those who do *us* wrong.

Third, we must experience *expressions of sorrow and forgiveness*. In families, we need to hear the words "I'm sorry" and "You're forgiven." We also need to have special signs that say, "We're back together again. Everything's okay." The Penitential Rite at Eucharist and the Greeting of Peace can be such occasions if we truly mean what we say and do.

When these experiences of love and forgiveness are woven through our daily family life, they enrich the occasions when we celebrate Reconciliation sacramentally. The two people in our imaginary samples above were probably able to approach the Sacrament because the three previous steps of the human reconciliation process were part of their lives. They will be strengthened to live out their resolves made within the

Sacrament because the basic human, family and community rituals of reconciliation will continue in their lives.

Children and the Sacrament

The Catholic parents who themselves value and celebrate the Sacrament of Reconciliation naturally want their children to celebrate it. This is a valid wish but, having worked a long time with Catholic families, I would offer some cautions here.

If parents who have this desire for their children do not avail themselves of the Sacrament regularly and in the spirit of the new Rite, then they should know that their children will only approach the Sacrament because they are told to do so. Their attitude toward the Sacrament will be the same as their parents'. Children learn their parents' attitudes by osmosis. And if they approach the Sacrament only because they are told, they will bring little to the Sacrament and take little from it.

The age when a child should first celebrate Reconciliation is an issue for Catholic families. Some Church officials have insisted that children should experience their first individual celebration of Reconciliation before receiving First Eucharist. This has not been universally accepted by all bishops in the United States. Those who choose to legally require the reception of Reconciliation before Eucharist often appeal to a statement in the *National Catechetical Directory* which says, "Reconciliation normally should be celebrated prior to the reception of First Communion" (#126).

Placing Reconciliation before Eucharist suggests that Reconciliation is a Sacrament of Initiation, which it isn't. Celebrating Reconciliation before Eucharist seems equally strange when considered in light of the theology of initiation, which says that only after one is fully initiated—that is, baptized, confirmed and a communicant—can one participate fully in the sacramental life of the Church. (The exception to this principle is a baptized person in danger of death.)

I do not mean to imply, however, that young children cannot and should not be called to an awareness of sin, forgiveness, conversion and God's mercy and reconciliation. The *National Catechetical Directory* also says:

Catechesis for the Sacrament of Reconciliation is to precede First Communion and must be kept distinct by a clear and unhurried separation. This is to be done so that the specific identity of each sacrament is apparent and so that, before receiving First Communion, the child will be familiar with the revised Rite of Reconciliation and will be at ease with the reception of the sacrament. (#126)

This statement immediately precedes the one above about the "normal" time for the reception of Reconciliation.

In my opinion, these statements present a clear incongruity. There is a distinct difference between children receiving catechesis about Reconciliation and being cognitively and spiritually ready to celebrate the Sacrament.

The Rite speaks of penance, conversion and reconciliation strictly in terms of adult experiences; there are no guidelines for applying the Rite to children. According to the Rite, the most important act of the penitent is "contrition" which it goes on to describe as *metanoia*—the "profound change of the whole person by which one begins to arrange one's life according to the holiness and love of God" (#6). I don't know about you, but I have a hard time seeing how any preadolescent can even begin to fulfill such a requirement. The practice of sacramental reconciliation for preadolescent children is one example of how the Church is caught in the tension between a former sacramental theology and a new theology in the early stages of growth, development and understanding.

In addition, as pointed out earlier, we may be making the old mistake of thinking, "We've always done it this way," when, in fact, the tradition of Reconciliation for preadolescents is only about 75 years old. Furthermore, the reception of Reconciliation is necessary only if one has committed grave (mortal) sin, and that is difficult to imagine in a seven-year-old.

In recent decades, developments in the area of psychology have brought up serious objections—which are also valid theologically—to the practice of Reconciliation for young children. We now know that children's moral development is a gradual process. Psychologists generally agree that few preadolescent children are able to make a distinction between moral wrong (sin) and violation of disciplinary regulations, between actions and motives for actions, and between rules and the reasons for accepting those rules. In short, preadolescents simply do not have the abstract reasoning ability or moral sophistication required for a theologically sound understanding of sin or the Sacrament of Reconciliation. Thus, they are hardly able to bring to the Sacrament the necessary conversion and reconciliatory experience.

Many psychologists and theologians caution against receiving the Sacrament too early because of the implications it can have. For example, if a child is at a stage of moral development where she perceives that what is wrong is what gets punished, the implication of confessing those wrongs could be a fear of punishment. She may further suppose that God is the one who punishes. If another child's moral reasoning tells him that wrongdoing makes him bad, the celebration of a Sacrament which includes confessing wrongs could contribute to a negative self-image. He may conclude that God couldn't possibly love a bad person. And, if still another child equates sin with the letter of the law without an understanding of the spirit of the law, the child could easily see the Sacrament of Reconciliation in terms of the old courtroom image we spoke of earlier. In each case, we expose the child to the danger of retarded moral growth.

Think back on your own moral development and attitude toward the Sacrament. Isn't it true that some of our negative attitudes toward the Sacrament were related to fear of punishment, legalism and a sense of unworthiness? Even after Vatican II renewed the theology of the Sacrament, many of us still experienced a retarded moral and spiritual development. We found ourselves making the same kinds of confessions as adults that we had made as children, accusing ourselves of the same types of sins: skipping prayers, being angry, eating meat, missing Mass, being unkind. It is very difficult to grow out of that morally immature concern with symptoms and to deal with real sinfulness, real conversion, real reconciliation.

Common Questions From Parents

So what's a parent to do? Having spent several years teaching all that is included in this book to parents interested in preparing their children for the Sacrament of Reconciliation, I know that there are several questions and concerns that parents have about children and the Sacrament. Following are some of the most common ones.

1) What's the best way to prepare my children for the Sacrament?

First of all, relax. You have been preparing them since the day they were born. You have been revealing to them a loving and forgiving God by being a loving and forgiving parent. You have been teaching the true meaning of reconciliation through your own family rituals and patterns of forgiveness and reconciliation. You have been sharing your faith with them, answering their questions, praying with them.

Statistical data and generations of common sense tell us that parents are the primary religious educators of their children. Schools and parish religious education programs merely affirm, support and build upon the faith you share with your children.

Look at your own attitude toward the Sacrament of Reconciliation. Your children will most likely adopt that attitude. If they see you approach the Sacrament with joy, and see you struggle with your own conversion and reconciliation, they will learn the realities of those complex and abstract principles from your actions. But, remember, it will be a gradual learning process; it won't happen overnight.

Take advantage of the preparation programs for the Sacrament that are offered for parents and children in most parishes. It is important to realize, however, that these programs are not designed to be instructional programs replacing the continuing and formal catechesis about the Sacrament for your children; nor do they replace the ongoing education and sharing that you do at home. They are primarily aids to help you do even better what you have been doing. They are tools to help the family focus on and celebrate the reconciling love it lives day by day.

2) Do my children have to approach the Sacrament of Reconciliation before First Communion?

No one, child or adult, is obliged to receive the Sacrament unless they are in the state of grave (mortal) sin. Church law stipulates that no one may be forced to receive any sacrament. While the *National Catechetical Directory* states that children should be exposed to, familiar with and prepared for the

Sacrament of Reconciliation prior to First Communion, it does not *mandate* that children receive those sacraments in that order. It says simply that Reconciliation is "normally," but not necessarily, received before First Communion. The child's and parents' choice and discretion always enter into consideration of whether or not the child should receive Reconciliation before First Communion.

At the same time, I would strongly recommend that parents invite their children to share with them in the parish communal celebration of the Sacrament of Reconciliation. Children can easily do this without availing themselves of sacramental absolution in the case of Form 2: Reconciliation of Several Penitents With Individual Confession and Absolution.

In cases where Form 3 is used — Reconciliation of Several Penitents With General Confession and Absolution — it is important to remember that this form *is* sacramental and can even serve as a child's first reception of the Sacrament of Reconciliation. Some families I've known have made this liturgically significant by notifying parish personnel ahead of time and arranging for the child to have a special role in the liturgy — such as being in the entrance procession, serving as Word bearer, or simply having his or her name announced during the service and being recognized as a first-time recipient of the Sacrament. A special reception might also be planned for the child after the liturgy.

However the Sacrament is celebrated, it is important to help your children understand that we celebrate it by one of three forms. Children should be familiar with all the forms, especially Form 1, so that when they are ready to approach the Sacrament in that form they will have some understanding of it.

In addition, it is a good idea for parents to show their children the parish reconciliation room. Children should also get to know the parish priests who may serve as their individual confessors. Introductions to both the space where the Sacrament may be celebrated and the presider of the Sacrament can contribute to a comfort and ease with the reception of the Sacrament when that time comes.

It could also be a good learning experience for parents to invite their children to accompany them when they use the individual form of the Sacrament. The parents could ask the children to wait in the church or chapel and pray for their parents while they are receiving the Sacrament. This can help children understand the communal aspect of sin and forgiveness as well.

3) Who decides when my children are ready to celebrate this Sacrament?

The Church holds that those who know the child best—the parents—should make this decision. Children, however, should also have some voice in this decision. Unless parents are certain that a child wants to receive the Sacrament only because of peer pressure ("Everyone else in my class is doing it"), the child's desire for the Sacrament should be respected. Just as one cannot be forced to receive a sacrament, one cannot be hindered from reception either. Especially in the case of Reconciliation, no one—no matter how close—can always be privy to the secrets of another's heart.

4) Isn't it important that children get into the habit of regular reception of the Sacrament of Reconciliation?

The answer to this question depends on what we mean by "regular." Our celebration of the Sacrament, as it is understood today, does not seem to call for the same once-a-month regularity urged by catechists and preachers of our recent past. Remember, the new Rite states that conversion—that "profound change of the whole person by which one begins to consider, judge and arrange his life according to the holiness and love of God"—is the most important act of the penitent. It would seem difficult for someone, adult or child, to bring such a "profound" and "whole" change of life-style to the Sacrament on a regular basis.

At the same time, it is important that children become familiar with and understand Reconciliation's invitation to growth, change and conversion. This can best be done if parents help children mark special moments in the lifelong conversion process with special celebrations as individuals, as a family and as members of the Christian community. If family reconciliation is celebrated normally and regularly at home—the main environment in which children grow, change and mature—children will understand the value of regular sacramental celebration as it is personally needed. In addition, if children see their parents publicly celebrating the Sacrament as a normal and regular part of life, they will follow the example.

5) What if my child is 16 and has never chosen to receive the Sacrament?

The only cases in which I have experienced such situations are in families in which there is no pattern of family forgiveness and reconciliation, or where the parents choose not to receive the Sacrament. If parents do not have a respect for the Sacrament and do not avail themselves of it, most children will follow suit. If, on the other hand, the parents do regularly receive the Sacrament, and there are regular rituals of family reconciliation, then the reluctant child may have a deeper problem that might warrant some professional psychological or spiritual counseling.

CHAPTER SEVEN

The Future of
Sacramental Reconciliation:
Personal Predictions

Earlier in this book I said that the Sacrament of Reconciliation has gone through several changes, and will probably go through even more changes as new needs surface. Predicting the future of the Sacrament could be a foolhardy endeavor. After all, who knows what future needs Christians may have for celebrating forgiveness? Who knows how future generations may choose to ritualize their experiences of reconciliation?

Still, one of the things we learned from Vatican II is that change in the Church, as in all of life and society, is constant. Change always follows need, and perhaps our greatest ongoing need as a Church is to be open to whatever reform our needs may call for in the future. We must take care that recent reforms do not get hardened into legalism, which, in turn, can blind us to the real needs of people. When that happens, growth stops, and one thing Christians cannot afford to do is stop growing.

Are more changes in the Sacrament of Reconciliation imminent? I would suggest that some are and, in fact, that some have already begun to happen. The following predictions about the future of the Sacrament are my own personal prognostications. Some theologians and liturgists are saying similar things about the Sacrament, even though they run contrary to the most recent statements of Pope John Paul II.

The Demise of Form 2

One of the changes I think we may see in the future is the demise
of Form 2: Reconciliation of Several Penitents With Individual
Confession and Absolution. This rite was basically a stopgap
measure developed because people were avoiding the
post-Tridentine Rite. It came out of people's immediate felt
needs and pastoral ministers' creativity. I believe that now that
we have taken the time to research the Sacrament, and have
come to a better understanding of its theology of reconciliation,
we are seeing that this form of the Sacrament appears to be
neither "fish nor fowl."

For one thing, it does not offer the relaxed, hospitable
environment required of the individual form of the Sacrament
because of the time element. A careful study of the ritual for the
individual celebration of the Sacrament suggests that the
penitent have time to do more than merely list sins, and that
the presider have time to do more than just listen, assign a
penance and "apply" absolution.

Yet this is essentially what occurs in the celebration of
Form 2. Usually in these services there are several "confessors"
to hear each person's serious sins, or the one sin he or she is
most sorry for, and then to assign a penance and give a quick
absolution. This practice is too much like a Word service that
we all sit through in order to procure a quick whitewash.

There is little time or opportunity for the affirmation and
encouragement toward continued growth that can be part of the
individual form.

At the same time, the communal aspect of this form of
the Sacrament is equally compromised. A major element of
communal Reconciliation is the supportive, accepting, forgiving
community welcoming the sinner home. But in Form 2, the
community simply seems to be there, not unlike the people with
whom we stood in line in the days of weekly and monthly
Saturday afternoon confessions. Instead of the community, the
confessors tend to become the center or focus in Form 2, because
they are the ones who hear our sins and "put us right" with
God. At most, the assembly sings and prays common prayers,
and perhaps exchanges a sign of peace.

The danger in Form 2, I believe, is having the bare essence
of both the individual and communal forms of the Sacrament

without having the real value of either—the chance to celebrate the conversion process we have experienced.

It sometimes seems that the main intent of such services is to provide a convenient way for parishes to handle individual holiday confessions. All the arrangements seem to be to that end: the services are most often offered during Advent and Lent; a number of confessors are at hand; clear directives are given for people to confess only serious sins; and efforts—usually musical—are made to hold people's attention while they wait for everyone to confess.

Those signs clearly say to me that the real goal of this form has become convenience. This is unfortunate because the original purpose of the communal penance services of the late 60's and early 70's was to respond to people's realization that, since sin affected the community, the community should be involved in forgiveness and reconciliation.

My experience with even the best-designed of these services is that, although the prayer, song, Word service and communal examination of conscience may be powerful and meaningful, by the time I wait for 100 people to confess their serious sins to four or five confessors, I become extremely restless. Sometimes I feel I should return to the confessor before the service is over! Recently, I've heard more and more people sharing my feelings.

The Total Acceptance of Form 3

When we see the demise of Form 2, I think we will see the other two forms, individual Reconciliation and communal Reconciliation with general absolution, come into their full, blazing life and power.

At this writing, Form 3—Reconciliation of Several Penitents With General Absolution—is only permitted by local bishops in cases of necessity. Some observers attribute the decision of Church officials to restrict this form of the Sacrament to fear that the experience of the communal form with general absolution will deter people from celebrating the individual form. This could happen, of course, if we do not provide adequate catechesis.

In my opinion, however, this fear is unwarranted. And

I suspect that there are other reasons for restricting this form, such as clinging to a more restrictive theology of sacramental action.

In my opinion, Form 3 meets a genuine need among Christians today: It makes visible and real the communal dimension of Reconciliation; it emphasizes that forgiving each other is our ministerial call. If we believe that every sin affects the community, then we must also believe that the community has to be involved in proclaiming forgiveness for sinners, aiding them to make new resolves, and helping them to live those resolves and assimilate their new grace into their daily lives.

What we really need—and what I think the future will bring—are better communal celebrations of the Sacrament of Reconciliation. Perhaps we need not only large services for entire parishes, but sacramental services for specific groups within the parish community. For example, family ministry or catechetical groups in a parish may gather for a special family Reconciliation service. There, family members could confess and reveal their conversion to one another and receive the forgiveness and reconciliation of each other and of the Church. The same could hold for other communities within parishes, such as prayer groups, social justice groups, renewal groups, parish committees and councils, and study groups. In addition, when there are parish divisions—which sometimes occur in human Christian communities—creative communal Reconciliation services can be extremely healing.

Something else I envision happening in the communal form of the Sacrament is more open and honest admission within the gathered assembly of our growth from sin to reconciliation. I'm not suggesting here just a listing of our sins in a kind of public confession, but a sharing with one another of the conversion journey which brought us to the celebration of Reconciliation. Such sharing can be both affirming to the sharer and encouraging to the rest of the assembly.

Revival of Individual Reconciliation

The community is only as healthy and reconciled as are the individuals in that community. As individuals experience more meaningful communal celebrations of Reconciliation, I believe we will gradually come to feel greater need for our own individual celebration of personal conversion and reconciliation.

The Christian community calls us to be spiritually whole and healthy individuals. The individual celebration of the Sacrament of Reconciliation can provide us with wonderful opportunities to stop and take personal stock of our spiritual lives. This is something, in my opinion, that every serious Christian would want to do at least once a year. If that happens, as it can, through the ministry of the Sacrament of Reconciliation, just imagine the possibilities for holiness in the Church and for spiritual power in the Christian community.

I also see the possibility of spouses or whole families using the individual form together. Every family experiences special moments of reconciliation and growth. A family could celebrate those moments sacramentally as a group by each participating in the individual form of the sacrament. Individual family Reconciliation can also be a beautiful way to introduce children to that form of the Sacrament. Possibly even close friends could use the individual form to celebrate together their special reconciliation experiences.

Nonordained 'Confessors'

Another aspect of the individual celebration of the Sacrament that I envision changing is that of confessing to an ordained minister. Actually, this is already happening. Nonordained pastoral ministers say that they regularly "hear confessions" but cannot give sacramental absolution. This will undoubtedly continue to happen because of the current and projected shortage of ordained ministers.

As a result, I see the stages of the Rite being celebrated separately rather than at one service: the confession and counsel possibly occurring at one time through the guidance of an unordained minister, and the absolution occurring later in a communal celebration with an ordained presider.

I suspect that if we look closely at our reconciliation experiences, many of us could say we have already confessed to a layperson—on retreats, in family rituals, with special friends, on Marriage Encounter or marriage enrichment weekends, with nonordained spiritual directors or in counseling sessions. Remember, "confessing to a layperson" or "soul friend" is not without precedent in our tradition. It occurred in scriptural times, in the early Church and even in the Monastic-Celtic era of the Sacrament's history.

A New Order of Penitents

At the 1983 Synod of Bishops, Cardinal Joseph Bernardin proposed a fourth Rite of Reconciliation modeled on the Rite of Christian Initiation of Adults. His idea is not new; it has been discussed widely by American liturgists for a number of years. In essence, his suggestion is a restoration of the ancient Order of Penitents, but without the stringent penances and public humiliation. I agree wholeheartedly with his recommendation and have seen it already implemented most effectively in parishes. It is a particularly meaningful ritual for alienated Catholics who are returning to the Church.

This new Rite might be structured in any number of creative ways. But, basically, it involves ritualizing the three C's of Reconciliation (conversion, confession, celebration) in stages over an extended period of time, such as Lent. Penitents may be assigned a "soul friend" or "sponsor" to journey through the stages with them. They may spend time searching their hearts and the Scriptures before confessing their sin and determining or accepting a penance. They can then have time to see if they can live their new way of life. Finally, when they are ready, they can celebrate their reconciliation with the Lord and the Christian community by receiving the absolution of the Church and returning to the Eucharist.

A ritual of this sort is increasingly needed in today's Church as we experience more and more the return of alienated Catholics. Yet it not only serves the returning Catholic, it also provides a powerful opportunity for the faithful to exercise their ministry of reconciliation. We would do well to consider this suggested new Rite seriously, and even be courageous enough to give it a try in our parishes.

Those are my personal projections or, better, personal hopes for the future of the Sacrament of Reconciliation.

A Final Word

Only we can make the Sacrament meaningful for ourselves. We can easily make excuses for not celebrating the Sacrament. Or we can reconsider our attitudes toward it, get rid of our "confession baggage," and come to a renewed understanding of its history, theology and potential for our lives. We will then see how "the old order" of sin "passes away" and we become "a new creation." And we will then know how to exercise more fully our communal ministry of reconciliation, forgiving as we are forgiven. As Reconciliation spurs us toward growth and fullness of life, we will be able to say with St. Paul, "Now all is new!"